Success guides

Intermediate 2
English

✗ Larry Flanagan ✗

Text © 2005 Larry Flanagan
Design & layout © 2005 Leckie & Leckie
Cover image © Caleb Rutherford

03/040108

ISBN 978-1-84372-285-4

Published by
Leckie & Leckie
3rd Floor
4 Queen Street
Edinburgh
EH2 1JE

Email: enquiries@leckieandleckie.co.uk
Web: www.leckieandleckie.co.uk

Special thanks to
Caleb Rutherford (cover design), Dorothy Comber (content review), Susan Moody (copy-edit),
The Partnership Publishing Solutions Ltd (page make-up), Hamish Sanderson (illustrations),
Roda Morrison (proofreading), Fiona Barr (index).

A CIP Catalogue record for this book is available from the British Library.

® Leckie & Leckie is a registered trademark

Leckie & Leckie Ltd is a division of Huveaux plc.

All websites referred to in this book were checked and were correct and working at the time of going to press.

Leckie & Leckie has made every effort to trace all copyright holders. If any have been inadvertently overlooked, we will be pleased to make the necessary arrangements.
We would like to thank the following for their permission to reproduce their material:
• The Random House Group Ltd for 'Touching the Void' by Joe Simpson, published by Jonathan Cape.

Leckie & Leckie would like to thank the following for permission to reproduce their copyright material without charge:
• 'Hotel Room, 12th Floor' by Norman MacCaig is reproduced by permission of Polygon, an imprint of Birlinn Ltd.
• The Herald newspaper and Sunday Herald for articles on pages 18–19, 21–23, 24–26.

Contents

Language

Literature

Personal study

Appendices

Welcome

Welcome to this guide to English at National Qualification Intermediate 2 level. It is designed to help you, the candidate, prepare and practise for your assessments during the course of the year and, in particular, to develop the skills you will need for the external examination in May.

English is an important subject for everyone. No matter what future career plans you have, a sound competence in English communication skills will be vital.

The skills involved in English – reading, writing and talking – are also crucial for further studies and whether you pursue these as a full-time student or as part of your employment, the ability to understand texts and tasks cannot be underestimated.

But English is important in its own right also. The study of literature, in particular, opens the door to understanding and making sense of the world in which we live and to determining our own sense of values and morality.

Hopefully this book will help you to achieve a good grade in your examination and also assist you to gain as much as you can from your English studies, in the widest sense possible. Learning is an active process, so try to engage with the activities offered.

A number of Scottish writers have been used in the exemplars and I hope you enjoy this aspect of the book. Although Scotland is a small country, we have much to say about the human condition.

The study of a Scottish text is compulsory, but there is no specific assessment task linked to this requirement.

I hope you find the book useful in pursuing your studies, and I wish you good fortune in all your efforts. But remember – the only place where success comes before work is in the dictionary!

Structure of the Course

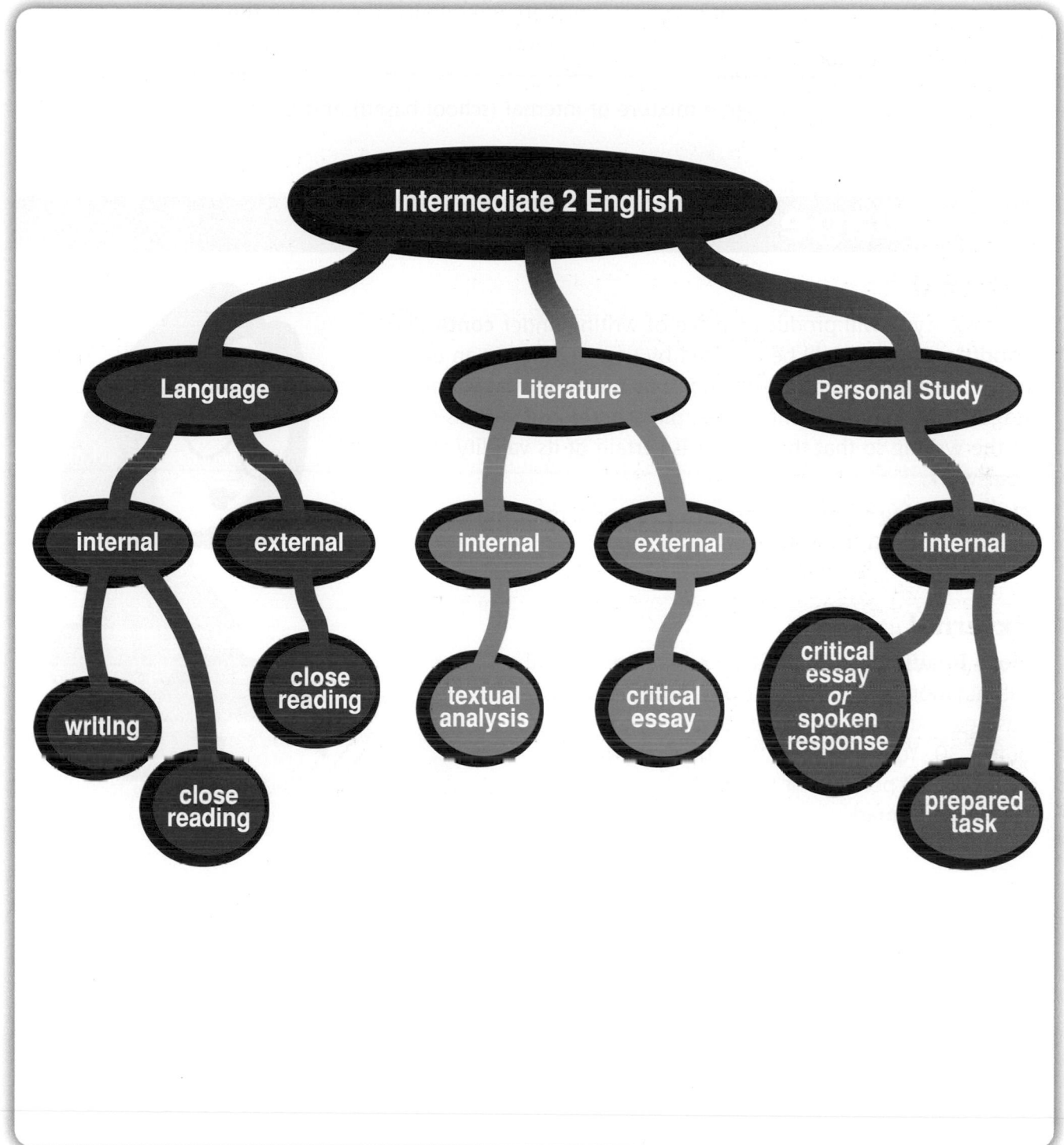

Course and assessment outline

Your course is organised into three units with each being allocated 40 hours of classroom study. In practice, however, the units are intertwined throughout the year, rather than being separate, as in some subjects. This lets you build up your skills base over the full session.

The course is assessed through a mixture of internal (school based) and external (the examination) testing.

Language

Internal

Writing – you will produce a piece of writing under **controlled conditions**, which will be assessed by your teacher as an end-of-unit assessment. Controlled conditions means that at various stages you need to submit a title, plan, notes and various drafts of the writing so that the teacher is certain of its validity as your work.

Close Reading – you need to pass (50 per cent or more) a Close Reading NAB for Unit Assessment purposes.

External

Close Reading constitutes Paper 1 in the external examination, which lasts for **one hour**. A single passage is used at Intermediate 2 and it is marked out of 30. Your mark will then be converted to count for 50 per cent of the final examination mark.

Literature

Internal

You will need to pass (50 per cent or more) a **Textual Analysis** NAB for Unit Assessment purposes.

External

Critical Essay is **Paper 2** in the exam, and you have **one hour and thirty minutes** for this section. You will attempt two critical essay assignments. These are marked out of 25 marks each, and together form a total of 50 per cent of the examination mark.

Personal study

Internal

You must produce a **critical essay (or spoken response)** on a **text** and **prepared task** of your own choosing. You write your essay under controlled conditions in one hour, using a maximum of two A4 pages of notes. In a spoken response, your talk will last for at least four minutes and you will need to be able to respond to questions from an audience of at least three people.

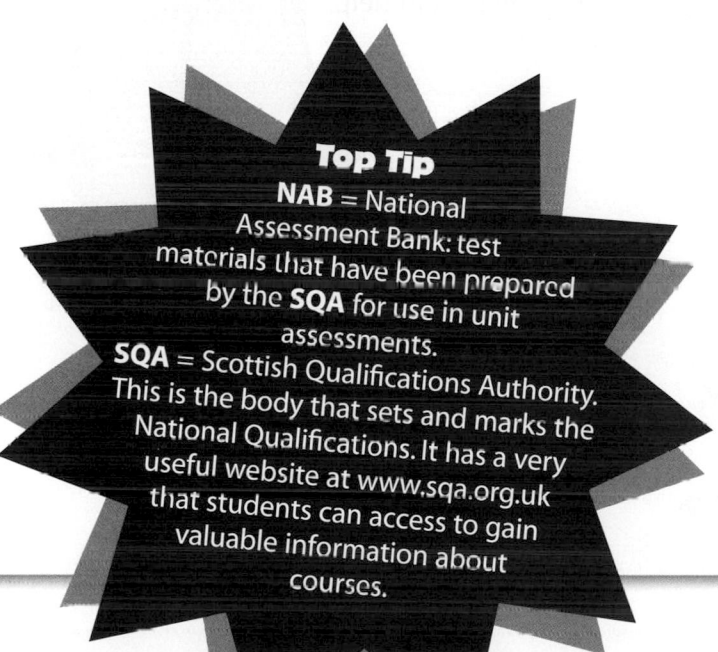

Top Tip

NAB = National Assessment Bank: test materials that have been prepared by the **SQA** for use in unit assessments.

SQA = Scottish Qualifications Authority. This is the body that sets and marks the National Qualifications. It has a very useful website at www.sqa.org.uk that students can access to gain valuable information about courses.

Close Reading

Introduction

Close Reading is an area you should be familiar with from Standard Grade or Intermediate 1. You need to build upon the base you have already established in terms of your close reading skills, demonstrating your ability to read and appreciate the detail and content of a text.

At Intermediate 2 you are looking to gain the equivalent proficiency of a Credit pass at Standard Grade. This will mean developing your skills in areas such as 'drawing an inference' and analysing language usage. Comparing Intermediate to Standard Grade, you will find that there are no new surprises, but the balance of the type of questions asked will change: there are fewer basic comprehension questions, for example, and more attention to an appreciation of the writer's craft and an evaluation of the writer's effectiveness.

Later in this book we will look at writing skills. Many of the suggestions that are made to improve your writing skills have equal application in improving your close reading skills. Learning about areas such as word choice, figurative language, topic sentences and paragraphs in terms of your own writing should help you see and understand the same techniques being used by someone else.

Top Tip

Making an inference is **understanding** something that is being suggested or hinted at in a text without it being explicitly stated.

Purpose of the assessment

The assessment is designed to test your ability to understand the **meaning** and **language** of a chosen passage. This will involve revealing an appreciation of not only **what** the writer is saying, but also **how** it is said.

What you will have to do

Close Reading assessments involve answering a series of questions on a single passage. These questions will cover three specific areas of close reading: **understanding (U)**, **analysis (A)** and **evaluation (E)**.

Understanding

Questions aimed at testing **understanding** will need answers that show an understanding of the passage's **key ideas**. You will be expected to identify important details and explain the main points of the text.

Analysis

In answering **analysis** questions, you will need to explain and comment on different examples of the passage's **structure** and **style**. You will need to examine how the language **shapes the meaning** of the writing and helps the writer to be clearer or more precise. Put more simply, this means looking, for example, at how the choice of a particular word might make the writer's intention clearer or how the use of brackets might affect the meaning of a sentence.

Evaluation

Evaluation questions ask you to decide on the effectiveness of a text, bearing in mind what the writer was trying to achieve. When you are answering these questions, it is helpful to use some critical terminology, and to think about the writer's purpose and stance. Relevant evidence from the text must be used to support answers.

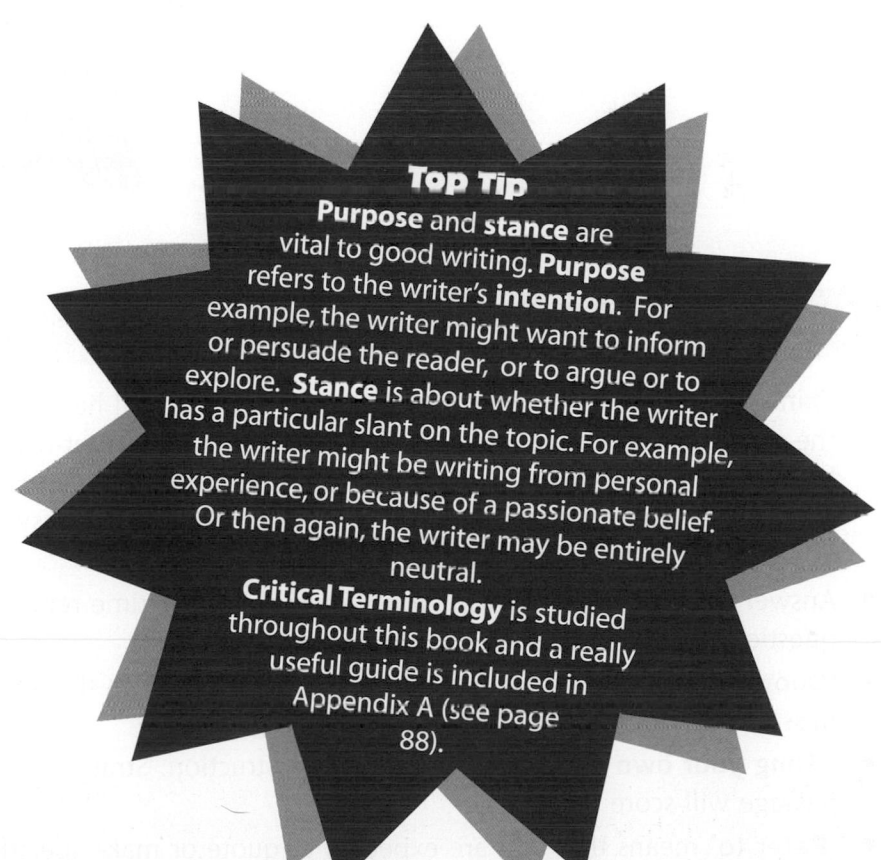

Top Tip
Purpose and **stance** are vital to good writing. **Purpose** refers to the writer's **intention**. For example, the writer might want to inform or persuade the reader, or to argue or to explore. **Stance** is about whether the writer has a particular slant on the topic. For example, the writer might be writing from personal experience, or because of a passionate belief. Or then again, the writer may be entirely neutral.
Critical Terminology is studied throughout this book and a really useful guide is included in Appendix A (see page 88).

How to tackle

Time

- Sufficient time **must** be allowed for reading the passage, as understanding the text is obviously the key to success. Passages will have been selected for use because they are of a difficulty and depth that require candidates to read them carefully.

- This will mean two readings of the passage. If one reading were all that was required, there would be little test of your abilities.

- During the first read, you should pay particular attention to the **topic sentences**. Topic sentences contain the **key messages** in a passage and provide the text with **structure**. You should be familiar with the role of topic sentences from your own writing. For more about topic sentences, see the section on 'Writing' (on page 36).

- After the first read through, look at the questions. The questions asked are an indicator of the important points within the passage.

- Finally, re-read the passage before beginning to answer the questions.

Top Tip

It is useful to familiarise yourself with the type of passages you may come across in the exam. The simplest way to do this is to read articles from good quality newspapers **regularly**. Sunday papers – for example *The Sunday Times*, the *Sunday Herald* and *Scotland on Sunday* – are often the best, and the magazine sections contain many well-written pieces that will help 'train' your mind.

Indicators

- Think about how to gain the **marks** on offer, as this will help you understand the nature of the answer to be given. For example, is a four-mark question looking for two points well made, or four brief points, or one key idea explored at length? Marks must be earned, so ensure your answer is appropriate to the value of the question.

- Answer as **directly** as you can. You should not waste time repeating the question in your answer.

- **'Quote'** means that you can lift the answer straight from the passage. Never miss out this type of question – if in doubt, guess!

- **'Using your own words'**, however, is an instruction. Straight 'lifts' from the passage will score zero.

- **'Refer to'** means that you are expected to quote or make specific reference to text from the passage.

Question codes

Be clear about what the questions are asking. After each one there will be a letter ('**U**' '**A**' or '**E**') indicating which skill area the question is testing. Make sure that your answer corresponds to the nature of the question.

- **Understanding** questions are concerned primarily with the meaning of the passage – what is being said by the writer.

- **Analysis** questions are more focused on how something is being said. These questions about language are often badly tackled because students do not respond to the actual question. For Analysis questions, you need to focus on the use of language (for example **tone**, the use of **metaphor** or **simile**, the order of the words within the sentence). These types of questions are not as difficult as they might seem.

- **Evaluation** is perhaps the most difficult area for many students. Questions here require you to have a holistic appreciation of the purpose and stance of the writer and within this context you have to judge the quality of the actual writing. (Holistic means having a sense of what the writer has been trying to do overall in the whole passage.) Although this is a subjective area, candidates have to justify their answer by reference to the text. It is essential, therefore, to link any comment and inference made to evidence from the passage.

Use the context

Be sure to read the introduction to the passage as it will indicate the source of the text – this should give you some idea as to the style/tone/purpose of the passage. For example, a passage from the travel section of book where the writer is recounting an experience is likely to be written in a conversational tone, with a good deal of personal anecdote involved. A passage aimed at persuading the reader about something, however, will be more forceful and will present arguments to support a particular viewpoint. The introduction helps us 'tune-in' to the passage.

Sentence structure

In sentence structure questions consider whether the sentence builds up to a climax, or whether it makes its key point at the start and then exemplifies it. Pay attention to the length of the sentence and the use of punctuation within it. Make sure you understand the use of different punctuation marks: colons, semi-colons, dashes, quotation marks, and so on.

Different types of sentences

Be aware of different types of sentences: Statement, Command, Exclamation, Question, and Rhetorical Question (a question that does not expect an answer).

Link question

The 'Link' question – when you are answering a question about linkage you need to identify how the word/phrase referred to links **back** to what has been said and also **forward** to what is going to be said. Do not write in generalities, however – deal with the actual ideas/content of the passage, quoting specific references as required.

Certain words indicate specific relationships between the sections being linked, for example:

- **yet** – this word introduces a reservation of some sort so you can expect that what is to follow will make some qualification to what has been stated already.

> The Scarlet Team is undoubtedly the best in Scotland. Yet it seems that the Amber Team will win the trophy.

- **but** – this word will introduce a contradiction, a change in direction, so you can expect that what follows will be the opposite of what has been said already.
- **and** – this word indicates an addition, a building up of the case already presented.
- **furthermore/in addition** – these words also indicate a building up of similar points.
- **consequently/as a result** – these words indicate that the events/problems/ solutions etc. that are mentioned after **consequently** or **as a result** are a direct result of what happened before.

Top Tip
By definition all links refer backwards and forwards but you must put flesh on this bone to gain the marks. Explain the link by referring to the actual detail of the passage.

You should also pay attention to the role of **pronouns** in linking questions. If you see the word 'this', for example, at the beginning of a paragraph, then it clearly is relating back to an idea from the previous paragraph and your task is to explain what that idea is and then identify how the writer develops or refutes that idea.

Remember that in a link question you must refer back and then refer forward, dealing with the specific ideas in the passage – you cannot have a one-sided link!

Length of answers

Where a question is worth a high number of marks (4-6 marks), you might find it helpful to write in short paragraphs or bullet points to be sure that you are developing your answer sufficiently to gain full marks.

Imagery

To answer imagery questions you must identify the image being used and then relate it to the ideas of the passage. Images are simply pictures/associations created in the reader's mind by the writer's use of language. Pay particular attention to effective **adjectives**, **adverbs** and **verbs** and to **figurative language** such as **similes**, **metaphors**, **personification**. Imagery questions are sometimes referred to as 'des & ref' – define the image and reference it to the ideas of the passage.

Understanding the question

Remember, when you are asked to 'refer closely to the passage' you are being asked to make a reference, i.e. **quote**. You must then comment on the reference as quotations alone rarely achieve a mark. Analysis questions in particular require quotation and comment.

Similarities and differences

You may be asked to comment on **similarities** and **differences** in the style of two passages. Consider areas of language such as formal/informal; factual/opinion; colloquial; personal/detached; journalistic; anecdotal; humorous/serious and so on.

Tone

Tone refers to the **attitude** being displayed. The **context** will help you decipher the tone being used. Try imagining the words being spoken – how would they sound? Some words that might describe tone are ironic, sarcastic, friendly, blunt, formal/informal, arrogant, nostalgic, regretful, angry, enthusiastic …

Use of inverted commas

Inverted commas are used:

- to indicate a **title** – for example 'Treasure Island' was written by Robert Louis Stevenson.
- to indicate when a **quotation** is being used – for example, one of the most well-known book openings was written by Charles Dickens: 'It was the best of times, it was the worst of times…'
- for **direct speech** – to indicate words actually spoken by a character or person – for example, 'You are a scoundrel, Sir,' exclaimed an irate member of the audience.
- to indicate when a word has **not** been used for its **literal meaning** – for example, 'This is my "gold" lad, honesty and trustworthiness – more valuable than any precious metal.'

Statistics

Students are sometimes mesmerised by statistics. The key issue is to think about the **point** being made by the statistic rather than simply thinking about the figure. Use the **context** to help understand the writer's purpose.

> One in twenty-five Scottish schoolchildren experience some form of dyslexic difficulty.

On its own this is merely a figure. In context you can be guided to a different understanding:

> As many as one in twenty-five Scottish schoolchildren experience some form of dyslexic difficulty – suggesting that this is a major problem.

> As few as one in twenty-five Scottish schoolchildren experience some form of dyslexic difficulty – suggesting that the scale of the problem is not significant.

Top Tip
Always think about why the writer has used a particular statistical example and seek to interpret his/her purpose.

Literal/non-literal

Words can be used in a **literal** and a **non-literal** sense. When a word is taken literally it means exactly what it says, for example, 'The knife edge was very sharp.' Sharp, here, means a cutting edge. If we said, 'The professor has a very sharp mind', we would be using a non-literal meaning for sharp - i.e. that the professor was very clever. The literal meaning would be that the professor's brain had a physical edge to it!

Evaluating effectiveness

When you are doing an evaluation question the answer does not lie in **what** your opinion is but in how well you **justify** that opinion.

Saying, 'The writer is very effective' or 'The writer is not effective' will score zero marks. The examiner wishes to see you justify your answer by making reference to the passage and by then making a sensible comment on the reference. Remember – reference alone always equals zero.

Word choice

In close reading assessments, you can take it as read that word choice will be a **key feature** of the questions. This may relate to testing your understanding of the meaning of words, or it may assess your ability to see the connection between words.

When seeking to understand the meaning of a word that you are not overly familiar with, use the **context** to help you derive the meaning. Is it connected by a 'but' to other words, for example, suggesting a contrast of some sort?

If you were to replace the word with something similar how would it impact on the meaning?

For example if someone 'strode' into a room it would be fair to assume that there was a certain sense of purpose about the character but if someone 'wandered' in, this might suggest a lack of clear purpose.

Top Tip

Context refers to the sentences/phrases around a particular word. It provides clues to the meaning of the word by creating some reference points for the reader.

Parenthesis

Parenthesis is the name given to the technique of **adding additional information** to a sentence. It is an important feature for a candidate to be able to spot as it often assists with working out answers.

Writers use parenthesis for a number of purposes: to supply additional information, to provide details or exemplification, to offer an aside or an authorial comment, to insert a reservation, to repeat an idea in a different style.

Parenthesis can be indicated in a sentence in a number of different ways:

- a pair of commas
- two dashes
- brackets
- sometimes by a comma/dash and a full stop.

Consider the following examples:

> John Fraser, Head Boy, stepped up to the lectern to make a speech of welcome.

Top Tip
Simply saying that the writer has used parenthesis is unlikely to gain a mark; saying why a writer has done so, or what impact it has had on a sentence, will.

The pair of commas indicate some additional information that helps us understand the context for the sentence a bit more.

> The Headteacher, known for her ferocity towards miscreant boys who wouldn't take a warning, moved towards the guilty two standing in the corner.

Without the parenthesis this sentence would read:

> The Headteacher moved towards the guilty two standing in the corner.

The writer has used the technique to add some spice to the setting by creating a particular atmosphere, creating a sense of anticipation on the part of the reader.

> He told me that I would be perfectly safe – somehow I didn't believe him – and that it was virtually unknown for this type of creature to attack human beings.

Here a pair of dashes has been used to indicate an aside from the writer that lets us see how he/she is really feeling.

When it come to analysing parenthesis try considering the sentence without the additional section and then see what is added when you include it.

Connotation/denotation

Connotation refers to the **associations** we make with words or phrases and **denotation** refers to the **specific literal meaning** of a word.

For example if we refer to something as 'cool' we can mean in strict terms that it is chilled (denotation) or we can be suggesting that it is acceptable, fashionable (connotation).

Simile/metaphor/personification

These figures of speech are often used to enhance the creativity and interest factor of a piece of writing. They involve drawing comparisons, direct or indirect, between two ideas/objects and are easily recognised. Once you have identified the comparison, deciphering the writer's meaning should be relatively straightforward.

Similes are direct comparisons, where the word '**like**' or '**as**' is used to link the two objects:

> My love is like a red, red rose that's newly sprung in June
> (Robert Burns)

Metaphors don't make a direct link; instead they **describe** one object **as if it was the other**.

> It is the east, and Juliet is the sun.
> (William Shakespeare)

Personification is a specific type of metaphor where an **inanimate object/idea/quality** is described as if it had **human qualities**:

> The heavy hand of fate slapped down the young pretender who was roundly beaten by the champion.

Pronouns

Pronouns are words used **in place of** nouns. Usually we would be told the **noun first** before a pronoun was used, for example:

> Bryan plays ice-hockey. He is often injured as it is quite a tough sport.

In this case we know that 'he' refers to Bryan. When a pronoun is used before we are aware of the noun, the writer is usually seeking to create dramatic impact by creating a sense of mystery or tension, for example:

> He had achieved fame and wealth before he was even a teenager. He is adored by tens of thousands of fans across the world. He has sold over a million albums and yet today he faces one of the biggest challenges of his life ...

By not revealing the person's name the writer is trying to entice the reader to read on and also creating a sense of anticipation about the identity of the person.

Words such as **he/she/it/they/these** are pronouns.

Close Reading practice

Introduction

The following passages are designed to help you develop your close-reading skills. They become progressively longer and more difficult as you move through them. Once you have tackled a passage use the answer guide to mark your work but study it also, to learn from any mistakes that you make.

Passage A

[Source – the *Sunday Herald*, 6 January 2005]

In the following article taken from the *Sunday Herald*, Jenifer Johnston reports on demands for UFO sightings to be given proper consideration. Read the passage and then answer the questions that follow.

Scientists argue it's time to take close encounters seriously ... no, seriously

If you've ever seen a little green man or lights in the sky, but were too afraid of the mocking that would accompany your confession, help is at hand.

5 A groundbreaking paper on the credibility of the UFO sightings has called for scientists to recognise accounts of contacts with other civilisations among the more outlandish claims of abduction and close encounters of the third kind.

It seems that Earth is in the midst of a "galactic habitable zone", with our sun being one of the younger stars within our galaxy.

10 Researchers argue in the paper, Inflation-Theory Implications For Extraterrestrial Visitation – published in the journal of the British Interplanetary Society – that older alien civilisations have enjoyed a billion year head start on us. If they exist, they will have had the time to unlock the secrets of physics and master time travel – and
15 they may well have visited Earth.

There are billions of stars in our galaxy, any number of which may have life-supporting planets orbiting them.

One of the authors, Dr Bruce Maccabee, told the
20 Sunday Herald: "This is a wake-up call for scientists. For years the scientific community has ignored possible sightings, which make it into the media purely as entertainment, but there is a high probability that some of them are genuine."

25 He and his co-authors point to Fermi's Paradox – if there are billions of planets in the universe capable of supporting life, and millions of intelligent species out there, then why have none visited Earth? – and speculate that recent developments in astrophysics,
30 biology, wormhole and superstring theories should allow scientists to

accept the possibility of UFO contact with humanity.

Maccabee compared the situation to that of conservationist Dian Fossey who made groundbreaking studies of gorillas, saying: "Alien civilisations may well have come to Earth and observed us rather
35 that interact with us."

Co-author Dr Bernard Haisch told the Sunday Herald: "Our best modern physics and astrophysics theories predict that we should be experiencing extraterrestrial visitation of such ... is scoffed at within our scientific community – either we are not being visited or we are
40 ignoring the visits. A few million dollars to methodically analyse accounts of UFO contact from around the world may throw up some interesting patterns and genuine accounts."

Both admitted that their scientific colleagues would find the proposal difficult to accept. Reports of abductions and grainy film footage of
45 spaceships have long been dismissed as wishful thinking, fabrications or even mental illness.

James Deardorff, lead author of the article said: "It would take some humility for the scientific community to suspend its judgement and take at least some of the high-quality reports seriously enough to
50 investigate ... but I hope we can bring ourselves to do that."

UFO hunter Ron Halliday author of several books on the subject, said a recognition of sightings is long overdue. "Scientists have had a very blinkered approach to UFO sighting in the past, and make it very difficult to even discuss anomalies with them, always taking them on
55 face value as fabrications. If you think about the potential for life on other planets it makes perfect sense that some of the accounts should be true."

Malcolm Robinson of Strange Phenomena Investigations who has studied accounts of UFO sightings over Bonnybridge – Scotland's
60 UFO capital – was also pleased with the research. He said: "The majority of UFO reports are explicable through natural events, but about 5% are inexplicable. They deserve proper investigation."

Graham Rule, secretary of the Astronomical Society of Edinburgh, said: "I would be of the view that if other civilisations existed
65 elsewhere in the universe, they may not exist any more. The light from the nearest stars to ours takes four years to get to us and it takes two million years to the nearest galaxy. Any messages that might have been sent in our direction could be very old indeed. As *The Hitch-Hiker's Guide To The Galaxy puts it* – space is really big. I
70 also have to think that if another life form was here and trying to contact us then why haven't they been more direct about it?"

Jenifer Johnston

Questions – Passage A

1 How does the writer create an informal tone in the opening
   paragraph (lines 1-3)?   1 (A)

2 What does the word 'credibility' (line 4) mean?   1 (U)

3 'Inflation-Theory Implications For Extraterrestrial Visitation' (lines 10-11).
   Why have capital letters been used here?   1 (U)

4 How effective is the imagery employed in the phrase 'wake-up call' (line 20)?   2 (A)

5 Consider lines 25-31.
   Using your own words, explain Fermi's paradox.   2 (U)

6 Consider lines 31-35.
   What is the point being made in the comparison with the study of apes?   1 (U)

7 Explain either use of punctuation in lines 38-39.   1 (A)

8 Consider lines 43-46.
   Using your own words, explain why earlier reports were dismissed.   3 (U)

9 Explain why it would require some 'humility' (line 48) for the scientists to
   'suspend its judgement and take some of the high-quality reports seriously...'   2 (U/A)

10 What is meant by the word 'inexplicable' (line 62)?   1 (U)

11 Consider lines 64-71.
    a. What is the general view of Graham Rule to the claims about alien
        visitors?   1 (U)
    b. Why does he hold this opinion?   2 (U)

12 Consider the passage as a whole.
    How effective do you find the final paragraph as a conclusion to the article?   2 (U/E)

Total = 20 marks

Passage B

[Source – *The Herald*, 5 January, 2005
(slightly abridged)]

In the following passage, taken from *The Herald* newspaper, Phil Miller argues
that it is time to re-assess the role of books in our society.

Let's not get emotional about books. It's time to bin them.

Nobody likes being proved wrong. Indeed, for months I had fought
with the idea of owning a digital music player. In a series of heated
conversations with more technologically-savvy friends, I repeatedly
argued that I just did not see the point. "But it's so brilliant, you can
5   listen to anything you want," one said, to which I replied "Why would
anyone want to carry around his entire collection of music all the
time?" The answer? "Because you can."

And now I do: I was given an iPod for Christmas and, indeed, it is
fantastic to carry around thousands of songs around with you. For a
10 music fan, it is liberating to be able to listen to whatever you want at
any time. Without doubt, the age of the invisible digital song is here,
and records, tapes and CDs are becoming history. Soon I wager,
following CDs down the road to oblivion, will be books. Not words, not
literature, poetry, prose or fact – but books.

15 There will be some upset over this. People are emotional about books.
They are still attached to them: to the feel of the binding, the calming
whisper of the turning pages, the sense of solidity, familiarity and
comfort. People feel complete by being surrounded by shelves of dusty
tomes, as if the contents of their educated minds were arranged
20 around them.

Certainly, reading in itself is not, thankfully, going out of style – book
shops are packed with customers. The market is large and expanding.

But I am sure the slightly nostalgic feelings of comfort and
familiarity for books was once felt about vinyl records, or in the past
25 20 years, the CD. However, vinyl is now collected by very few people
– and vinyl bores, really are as tedious as car bores or wine bores.
The number of collectors is bound to dwindle further, while compact
discs are being rendered irrelevant, every time somebody downloads a
song from the internet – which they do in their millions. The book
30 will go, eventually, the same way as the CD is – after all, there are no
bookshelves in Star Trek are there?

To be honest, I will not shed a tear. The book is the medium, not the
message, and as a medium, it is flawed. The message – prose, poetry,
words, literature – will never die as long as civilisation exists. Indeed,
35 they are essential for our society. But the day of the book is
numbered. For a start, books are highly perishable: they rip, tear, get
drenched, can burn (stacks of books are kindling for many a house
fire), become damp, dusty, mouldy and smell. They also take up far
too much room – shelves and shelves of never read, once-read, or
40 seldom-read books glower at you day and night.

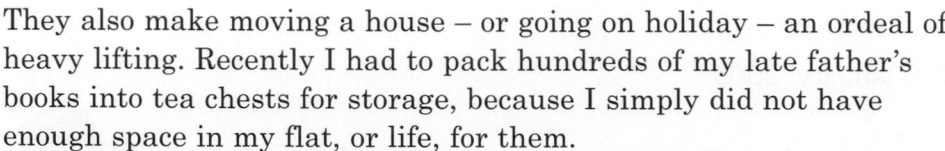

They also make moving a house – or going on holiday – an ordeal of heavy lifting. Recently I had to pack hundreds of my late father's books into tea chests for storage, because I simply did not have enough space in my flat, or life, for them.

45 But as box after box disappeared into storage, I realised I would never, in reality, have read them again. And how many books do you really re-read, over and over again? Not my dad's 28-volume history of the Boer wars, that's for certain.

I'm not, of course, suggesting a mass burning of books is in order, a
50 Fahrenheit 451-style immolation – although if someone could devise a way of turning books, all those useless unread books, back into trees the world would be a better place – but gradually reading and purchasing habits will change. In the near future, the humble book will be as antiquated as the wax cylinder is now.

55 Already many young people read more words on the internet than they do on paper. More books should be available on the net, although thousands are already. There will be cheap, small, transportable screens which you can carry in your handbag or pocket, with which you will be able to access your own personal library. "eBook" reading
60 devices are already on the market.

Instead of buying a book, you can download and read it with your personal screen technology. You could swap books with friends with the simple use of a cable. Technology always fills (and creates) demand – and people will want easier, simpler, more accessible
65 literature, prose, poetry and words.

With iTunes, buying a single song costs 79p. Perhaps buying a single poem will be at the same price. Chapters in books could be bought as you read them, and the authors would circumnavigate publishers (and agents) and sell their words direct through a digital connection –
70 á la Stephen King.

Whole libraries could be transferred in seconds, classic after classic uploaded to computers and hand-held readings screens across the globe. You could carry the entire works of Shakespeare in your pocket. Or the entire Harry Potter series, if you really wished.

75 Bibliophiles will become as quaint as members of the Flat Earth Society or, perhaps more accurately, real-ale aficionados. After all, owning books does not make you a wiser, kinder or more intelligent person: I have met plenty of people with row after row of books in their house – who are as ignorant and foolish as anyone who has never read. A
80 large personal library, in itself, is no guarantee of anything – apart from impressive shelving. Reading, however, improves, enriches and engorges the mind and creates a more educated, cultured society: so the easier and quickest access there is to the worlds of literature and thought, the better.

85 What is plain is that the process of digitising literature should be speeded up forthwith, in all the fields – in education institutions, in libraries, in business, on the internet and from book shops. Books will

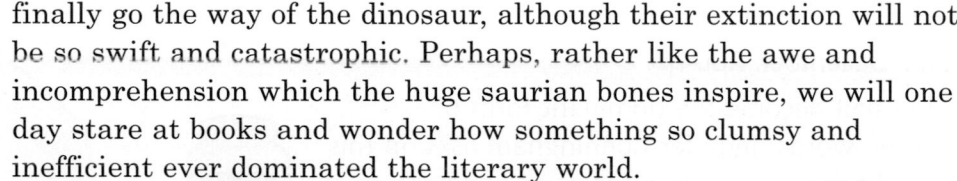

finally go the way of the dinosaur, although their extinction will not
be so swift and catastrophic. Perhaps, rather like the awe and
90   incomprehension which the huge saurian bones inspire, we will one
day stare at books and wonder how something so clumsy and
inefficient ever dominated the literary world.

Phil Miller

Questions – Passage B

1 The writer establishes an informal tone in the opening paragraph.
Explain two of the ways in which this is done.   2 (A)

2 'Nobody likes being proved wrong' (line 1).
In what way was the writer proved wrong?   2 (U)

3 Explain the writer's use of a colon in line 16.   1 (A)

4 How does the context help you understand the meaning of the phrase
'vinyl bores', (line 26)?   2 (U)

5 'The book is the medium, not the message' (lines 32-33).
Quote a phrase from earlier in the passage that contains the same idea as this
expression.   2 (U)

6 Using your own words, explain why the writer feels that 'the day of the books is
numbered' (lines 35-36).   2 (U)

7 'I simply did not have enough space in my flat, or life, for them' (lines 43-44).
What does the writer mean by this expression?   2 (U)

8 Consider lines 49-54.
What would the writer see as being a useful outlet for old books?   1 (U)

9 Consider lines 55-70.
   a What evidence is there that the writer's ideas may be actually happen?   1 (U)
   b What can you deduce about Stephen King from the passage?   1 (A)

10 'if you really wished' (line 74).
What does the inclusion of this phrase suggest about the writer's attitude to
Harry Potter books?   2 (A)

11 Consider lines 75-84.
Explain the difference between owning books and reading, as suggested
by the writer.   2 (U)

12 Why has the writer used a dash in line 86?   1 (A)

13 How effective do you find the comparison made in the final sentence
(lines 89-92)?   2 (A/E)

14 Referring to the passage as a whole, how persuasive do you find the
writer's argument?   2 (E)

Total = 25 marks

Passage C

[Source – *The Herald*, 11 December, 2004]

As mobile phones and e-mail become the dominant form of communicating our written words, Jennifer Cunningham asks, in this slightly abridged article, if there is any place for good handwriting in a technological society.

Handwriting ... is it worth the paper it is written on nowadays?

Learning to write legibly is hard work for most five and six year olds. Some children don't even get the hang of it by the end of primary school. But when almost every teenager in the land is nimbly thumbing text messages to friends while simultaneously
5 holding a conversation with someone else, do they really need to learn to write things down neatly on paper anymore?

The English Language 5-14 document, which all schools follow as the basis for their language policy, sets attainment targets for handwriting and presentation which state that pupils should "form letters and space
10 words legibly" at the basic level, to "employ a fluent, legible style of handwriting, and set out completed work clearly and attractively" at the top level.

It's not just the teachers who defend such an approach. In fact, a society in which the hand-written word was reduced to little more than
15 notes and shopping lists and, with luck, the odd brilliant idea noted down on the back of an envelope, would be cause of disquiet to many.

"Children most definitely need to acquire handwriting skills," says Dr Patrick Dixon, as an analyst of where global trends are leading. "Although we increasingly depend on technology, it is always more
20 convenient to make a spontaneous note on a piece of paper that happens to be at hand than fire up an electronic device and get it to the right programme. I predict that young people will still be writing notes in 20 and 30 years' time, although they will also need keyboard skills."

Dixon himself admits that his own use of the keyboard means he can
25 no longer write at speed and suggests that in the future, it may well be the case that students will be given the option of typing out their answers in exams, which at the moment test an ability to write quickly as well as other skills of knowledge and mental agility.

Equally convinced that children need to master the ancient art of
30 handwriting is Morag Russell, a senior lecturer at Aberdeen University. "We recommend to students that children should have regular handwriting practice up to Primary 7," she says.

"At the early stages, it is absolutely vital for the teacher to observe how the children form letters, because, although a letter may look right, if it
35 has been formed incorrectly, there will be horrific problems for children to join it up.

"What everyone agrees on is that where children have difficulties with writing, they have difficulties with spelling, because they are

40 expending so much energy on writing they cannot think about other things like spelling or meaning. There is a strong connection linking writing, spelling and thinking."

Russell describes the idea that computers will make handwriting redundant similar to the argument that books would be overtaken by television and computers. "We still read books and we don't need to
45 plug in a machine to write a shopping list," she says, while singing the praises of a computer based writing programme for which children use the equivalent of an electronic blackboard.

Schoolchildren in Fife are taught a script based on a 1998 design by the doyen of handwriting in Scotland, Tom Gourdie. At the age of 91 he
50 confesses he was, "a wee bit disappointed" that it had not been adopted as the basis for teaching handwriting throughout Scotland, simply because of his profound belief that "it is extremely important for children to learn to write in a simple, practical, calligraphic style."

He himself remembers wishing he had been taught better at school.
55 "When I was small, I learned to write on a slate and I hated the scraping. Later I asked the art teacher for help, but it was only at Edinburgh College of Art that I discovered calligraphy."

Children are still being failed, he says, citing the case of a pupil about to sit his Highers at an Edinburgh fee paying school, who wrote saying
60 that he feared any letter of application for a job would be ignored because of his handwriting.

"It's not the teacher's fault, because they have not been taught to write properly. I would like Scottish schools to take writing more seriously, because I get letters from all over the world from people who want to
65 improve their handwriting."

Other countries have developed different solutions from the UK. In France, where letter-writing has not been replaced by the telephone to the same extent as in Britain, schools continue to teach a single national style of cursive handwriting and it continues to have a high
70 school priority in French primary schools.

French teachers and educational professionals have a considerable degree of knowledge of the principals underlying the teaching of handwriting and exercises in art and PE are designed to link with the teaching of handwriting. Children spend more time on writing than
75 reading between the ages of three and eight, and teachers believe that fluent handwriting "unlocks the mind".

Applications for jobs and even replies to classified ads are usually by letter, whose construction, handwriting and presentation are fully expected to be carefully examined.

80 Such a close concentration on handwriting is what experts in this country want.

Christopher Jarman, who devised a script very similar to Tom Gourdie's for use in London schools argues, "You just have to go into any bookshop and look at the vast number of books on calligraphy to

85   see that there is a whole new interest in handwriting as a leisure and craft activity as well as a functional one. I've retired now, but never a week goes by without a request from someone about how they could improve their handwriting. I've just had one from a couple who are both doctors."

90   Perhaps they – and Scotland's schoolchildren – should remember the case of the drug thief who was caught when he presented a prescription to a pharmacist, who decided it was far too legible to have been written by a doctor. Perhaps he was just too well taught.

Jennifer Cunningham

Questions – Passage C

1   Consider the opening paragraph.
    a What evidence is offered to support the idea that children find learning to write difficult?   1 (U)
    b Explain the writer's use of the word 'But' in line 3.   2 (A)
    c How does the writer's choice of language underline the ease with which teenagers can text?   2 (A)
    d Why has the writer posed a question at the end of paragraph one?   1 (A)

2   'form letters and space words legibly' (lines 9-10).
    Explain how the context helps you understand the meaning of the word 'legibly'.   2 (U)

3   Consider lines 17-28.
    a Dr Dixon feels that writing will continue to be more popular than using technology for everyday use. How does his choice of language support this idea?   4 (A)
    b How does he see the future developing for writing in general?   1 (U)

4   Consider lines 29-47.
    a 'master the ancient art of handwriting' (lines 29-30)   2 (A)
       Comment on the language used in this expression.
    b How might poor handwriting create other difficulties for pupils?   1 (U)
    c Explain the comparison made between computers and televisions.   2 (U/A)

5   Consider lines 48-65.
    a Quote an expression that suggests that Tom Gourdie is regarded as an expert on handwriting.   1 (U)
    b Explain the connection between the anecdote about his own school days and that of the Edinburgh school pupil.   1 (U)

6   Consider lines 66-79.
    a Using your own words, list four of the ways that the situation in France differs from that in Britain.   4 (U)
    b 'unlocks the mind' (line 76).
       How effective do you find this image?   2 (A/E)

7   Consider lines 80-89.
    What evidence is provided to support the claim that there is still an interest in handwriting?   2 (U)

8   How effective do you find the final paragraph as a conclusion to the article?   2 (E)

Total = 30 marks

Passage D

[Source – *Times Educational Supplement*, 7 November 2003]

In this article Lynne Truss, author of the best-selling book *Eats, Shoots and Leaves*, puts the case for paying more attention to punctuation.

Dash it – isn't it time the dot gone generation got the point of punctuation?

A panda walks into a cafe and orders a sandwich. He eats the sandwich and seems to be behaving in a fairly ordinary panda fashion until, instead of paying the bill, he produces a gun, fires at the waiter and strides towards the door. "Why?" cries the wounded
5 man, as the panda passes. "Because I'm a panda; look it up," replies the panda enigmatically, tossing a wildlife manual on the counter. The waiter consults the manual and immediately discovers the grammatical cause of this strange behaviour. "Panda," says the tragically ill-punctuated entry. "Large black-and-white bear-like
10 mammal native to China. Eats, shoots and leaves."

There are, I believe, many versions of this joke but the excellent news I had when I first proposed "Eats, Shoots & Leaves" as the title for a book on the history and future of punctuation is that it is a joke *told by children in playgrounds*. This was reassuring. Because if people of
15 pre-adult age can appreciate the comic value of a misplaced comma may there not be hope after all for this seemingly arbitrary set of dots and squiggles that have decorated the printed page for the past 500 years?

Things have not been looking good lately, you see. While the National
20 Literacy Strategy is now trying to rectify matters, 30 years of anti-grammatical, education practice has seen to it that – well, look around these days for the comma, the apostrophe, the hyphen, and what you will find is a system of quite simple and helpful conventions being held in general contempt.

25 Punctuation, however, has been around for as long as there has been writing. It was originally devised as a system to indicate to Greek actors where to pause for breath, and this function as a kind of musical notation for reading aloud kept it going for 1,500 years.

But its authority with respect to grammar derives from printing.
30 Printers in the 16th and 17th centuries invented the convention of the apostrophe to represent letters omitted ("can't", "won't"); they also came up with semicolons, colons, full stops, commas, quotation marks and dashes. Punctuation both illuminates grammar and indicates tone and rhythm, but its all-important purpose is very simple: to
35 avert misunderstanding and make things easier to read.

Nowadays the big problem is the apostrophe. There are those who cry out for its abolition on the pragmatic grounds that no one knows how to use it any more. And there are others (with whom nowadays I find myself increasingly allied) who choke and splutter and take digital pictures of illiterate signs outside petrol stations and send them off to the website of the Apostrophe Protection Society (there really is one), so that a great wail of "Aieee" can go up from all the other people likewise sent into paroxysms by apostrophe misuse in public places.

Sensible language experts such as David Crystal reckon that we are watching the terminal, dazzling burn-out of the apostrophe: we should just sit back and observe the phenomenon through a bit of tinted glass. Language is a living thing, after all; it always sorts things out in the long run. But it's hard for those of us who are susceptible to the "Aieeee!" and rock-throwing response when we see seemingly well-educated people not knowing their *its* from their *it's*, because it means stupidity is winning.

A few years ago it might have been fairly argued that the niceties of punctuation were the province of only writers and editors; the rest of us didn't need to know. But a funny thing has happened to the written word in the past few years. It has exploded. Everyone's a writer. Moreover, with the internet, everyone's an editor and publisher as well. And it now seems a rather cruel trick that a whole generation was sent out into the world without the simplest notion of how to write a sentence.

In the 1960s, when dastardly educationists decided that grammar was a silly old-fashioned thing, I believe there was a hazy idea of the immediate future as a benignly post-literate place in which the ability to construct a sentence would be faintly remembered as an ancient (lost) technique akin to mixing woad or fashioning arrow-heads out of bits of flint. They really thought the written word was on the way out, and that verbal self-expression could be better achieved if you removed the very means by which we verbally express anything at all. Whereas in fact (nobody could have anticipated this), it was the *printed* word that was on the way out. In what historians of the future will doubtless call "a bit of a turn-up", along came the internet, email and the mobile phone, to challenge traditional forms of writing and reading, and provide a global verbal forum for anyone with a keyboard and a telephone line. The language of the internet encourages an almost anti-grammatical approach to language, with words run together (or separated by "dots"); meanwhile, email acceptably adopts the anti-grammar of self-important haste, neglecting initial capitals, using exclamation marks a lot (!) and linking phrases with the dash (–) or the ellipsis (…)

However, the plucky little marks are still going, despite all the onslaughts. They are not dead yet. Given half the chance, the apostrophe still flits about like Tinkerbell, rescuing a bizarre sentence such as "Prudential: were here to help you." By making it clear that it's actually "Prudential: we're here to help you." The ever-willing comma chases round the hillside of language like an over-eager sheepdog, herding words into the right pens, so that a notice

that says "No dogs please", (an indefensible generalisation, since
most dogs rather make a point of it) is properly rendered "No dogs,
please". The muscular colon and semicolon provide internal energy to
long sentences containing complex thoughts; and the manly dash –
90 like this – lifts separable phrases quite clear of the surrounding
prose, using both hands and a considerable power of push.
Exclamation marks and question marks provide tone of voice. Italics
provide instant *emphasis*. Brackets do their (isn't it marvellous?)
bracketing thing. Meanwhile the indispensable hyphen makes sure
95 that unpronounceable words such as *shelllike* and *deice* emerge
clearly as *shell-like* and *de-ice*. Finally, as for the wonderful ellipsis
(or three dots) . . . what can I say?

I discovered in researching the history of punctuation, incidentally,
that I was in love with the colon. I had no idea this would be the
100 result, and I haven't told anybody this before, but actually I always
fall in love with a character in my books, and by the end of *Eats,
Shoots & Leaves* I adored the colon and wanted to have its babies. On
which bizarre note (sorry), here are two letters which show just how
thoroughly we rely on punctuation.

105 *Dear Jack,*

*I want a man who knows what love is all about. You are generous,
kind, thoughtful. People who are not like you admit to being useless
and inferior. You have ruined me for other men. I yearn for you. I have
no feelings whatsoever when we're apart. I can be forever happy ~ will*
110 *you let me be yours?*

Jill

Dear Jack,

*I want a man who knows what love is. All about you are generous,
kind, thoughtful people who are not like you. Admit to being useless*
115 *and inferior. You have ruined me. For other men I yearn! For you I
have no feelings whatsoever. When we're apart I can be forever happy.
Will you let me be?*

Yours, Jill.

Questions – Passage D

1 Why does the writer use the word 'tragically' in line 9?   2 (U)

2 Consider lines 11-18.
   a Explain the writer's use of italics in lines 13-14.   1 (A)
   b In what way does the writer find the reaction of children to the joke
      to be 'reassuring' (line 14)?   2 (U)

3 Using your own words, explain the reason for the 'general contempt' referred to by the
   writer in line 24.   1 (U)

4 What does the writer mean by referring to punctuation as a kind of 'musical notation',
   (line 28)?   2 (U)

5 Consider lines 29-35.
   For what main reason did printers devise the various punctuation marks?   1 (U)

6 Consider lines 36-43.
   a How does the context help you understand the meaning of the word
      'pragmatic' (line 37)?   2 (U)
   b Comment on both the structure and the language of the sentence
      'And there are ... public places' (lines 38-43).   4 (A)

7 How effective do you find the imagery used in lines 44-47?   2 (E)

8 Explain the full meaning of the word 'exploded' (line 55).   2 (U/A)

9 Consider lines 60-78.
   a How does the writer's word choice in the opening sentence mock the
      ideas of the 1960s?   2 (A)
   b Explain the impact of new technology on language use.   2 (U)
   c What criticism of internet language does the writer make?   2 (U)

10 Consider lines 79-97.
   Choose one of the images linked to a specific punctuation mark and explain
   how effective the writer has been in using the image to make a point.   2 (A)

11 Comment on the tone of lines 98-104.   1 (A)

12 How effective do you find lines 105-118 as a conclusion to the article?   2 (E)

Total = 30 marks

Answers – Passage A

1   Comment could be made about either the humour of 'little green man' or the stereotypical absurdity of the image.
    A mark could be gained also for a gloss on the word 'mocking', suggesting a light-hearted approach.
    NOTE – reference alone scores zero.

2   Accept 'truth' or 'likelihood' or similar explanation.

3   It is a title.

4   Root image is that of an alarm waking someone up from sleep, suggests that the scientists have been metaphorically sleeping and unaware of the potential truth of some sightings.

5   That because of the scale of the possibilities of life on other planets, you would expect that some contact would have been made by now if anything actually existed.

6   That other species may have studied us without disturbing us, in the same way that the apes referred to were studied.

7   Ellipsis, ..., used to suggest that some additional detail has been missed out. Dash used to add an additional comment by way of explanation.

8   Hopeful desires, lies or untruths, mental instability.

9   Humility is the act of being able to accept gracefully that you were wrong; scientists have been certain that they were right and would have to admit to their errors.

10 Cannot be explained.

11 a   That if aliens did exist, they are probably extinct by now.
    b   The speed at which communications can travel, coupled with the distance to other galaxies, would mean that any signal we receive would be ancient and the senders no longer living.

12 Candidates are free to argue for or against effectiveness but some reference to the ideas contained in the passage must be made.

    Possible answers might refer to the slightly downbeat negative tone as linking with the opening humour and scepticism, thereby rounding the article off but in a slightly more serious tone. Equally, candidates may refer to the weight of the article being supportive of the idea of aliens visiting earth, various quotations from scientists, so ending with a quotation that does not support the idea creates a balance to the article.

Answers – Passage B

1   Reference to the colloquial use of 'savvy' and the use of dialogue.

2   He now owns an I-pod and also that he likes/admires it.

3   After the colon he gives examples of the ways in which people are attached to books.

4   Reference to the words 'tedious', meaning tiresome and repetitive leading to the meaning of 'bore' as something uninteresting.
Also accept reference to the further examples of 'bores' as people who talk at length on a subject without interesting the listeners.

5   'Not words, not literature, poetry, prose or fact – but books'

6   Reference to: 'highly perishable' suggesting that they are easily destroyed. 'take up far too much room' – idea of too bulky, requires excessive storage and so on.
NOTE – reference alone scores zero.

7   Physically not enough room to store and either emotionally (because of personal connection to his Dad) or intellectually he wished not be associated with them.

8   That they could be recycled back to nature – help grow more trees.

9   a   The suggestion that children read more on the internet than they do from books.
    b   That he has published books on the internet.

10   Slightly dismissive tone suggests that the writer doesn't think that anyone would or should want to do this; suggests that he doesn't rate the books very highly.

11   Owning books relates to the physical acquisition of them and this might be only for display purposes with the owners be no wiser as a result; reading them refers to the idea that the books are studied and their content absorbed, leading to more understanding and knowledge.

12   Introducing examples of 'all the fields' mentioned before the dash.

13   Answers are likely to refer to the idea of dinosaur bones, an image of the past that still commands our respect and admiration. Suggesting that in the future people may look back on books, which will be 'extinct' by then, with the same feelings. Effective summary to the passage's main argument.

14   Requires to be marked on merit but points made must be referenced to the passage.

Answers – Passage C

1   **a**   *Reference should be made to the fact that even by the end of primary not all children have mastered the skill of writing.*

        b   *'But' links the contrast between the difficulty with writing and the ease of texting.*

        c   *References: 'nimbly' suggesting quickness, agility; 'simultaneously' suggesting ease as person can multi-task while texting.*

        d   *Posing a question that will then be addressed in the remainder of the passage.*

2   *'legibly' means clearly, readable. Context talks about forming and spacing letters, suggesting that they are shaped properly; also refers to 'fluent' suggesting clear flow, skilful.*

3   **a**   *He uses the words 'always more convenient' and 'spontaneous' referring to handwriting, suggesting that the ease and naturalness with which we can write will aid its popularity.*
           Conversely, in referring to technology he uses the image of firing up a device, suggesting a starting process being required, and then the need to search for the right programme – all of which suggests a slower more cumbersome process than that outlined for writing.

4   **a**   *Solemn, serious, respectful tone; references 'master' as in a serious skill, 'ancient' as in old, revered.*

        b   *Concentrate on writing so much that their brain doesn't deal properly with other areas like spelling and thinking.*

        c   *People thought that television would be the end of books but they were wrong; similarly those who think that computers will be the end of handwriting are equally wrong.*
           For full marks candidates must get the idea that both assumptions are wrong.

5   **a**   *'doyen of handwriting'*

        b   *He felt that school failed him in relation to his handwriting and the Edinburgh pupil feels the same.*

6   *Acceptable gloss on four of the following:*
     'letter-writing has not been replaced by telephone'
     'schools continue to teach a single ... style of cursive handwriting'
     'continues to have a high priority in French primary schools'
     'French teachers ... have a considerable degree of knowledge...'
     'exercises in art and PE ... link with the teaching of handwriting'
     'children spend more time writing between ... three and eight'
     'teachers believe that fluent handwriting "unlocks the mind"'
     Straight lifts score zero.

7   *Root of image – idea of a locked door being opened. Effective because it suggests that fluent handwriting opens up the mind to thinking (ideas and thoughts).*

8   Reference to the number of books on the skill of handwriting and the fact that Jarman is continuously receiving letters asking for help with handwriting.

9   Mark on merit but comments should be justified by some reference back to the passage.

Humorous anecdote to finish – stylistically effective as the passage has had a light tone to it throughout.

Ironical illustration of the content of the passage and the importance of handwriting.

Echoes comments in the passage about the importance of teaching and education.

Answers – Passage D

1   Tragic as in fatal; mistake led to death of waiter.

2   **a**   To emphasise her surprise that children were telling the joke.
     b   She thinks that it is good to see children understand the use of the comma, and this gives her hope for the future of punctuation generally.

3   Essentially that it was out of fashion to teach grammar in schools and therefore people are generally ignorant of its importance.

4   In the same way that notation on a music script helps the musician understand and play the piece, so punctuation helps the reader to understand what is being said.

5   To make the printed word easier to understand.

6   **a**   'Pragmatic' means practical, realistic; the context refers to the fact that no one knows how to use it properly so it would be more straightforward to abolish it.
     b   Possible references:
- use of parenthesis to make authorial comment
- begins with a conjunction
- use of connectives to create sense of breathless indignation
- language: colloquialism of choke and splutter
- 'aieee'
- paroxysms

For full marks both structure and language must be covered, but not necessarily equally. Up to two marks for reference and sensible comment. Reference alone scores zero.

7 Image is that of a shooting star; linked to idea of 'terminal' as in dying away suggests that the apostrophe is also dying out. Candidates are free to comment on effectiveness – may endorse image as in keeping with the attitude of the writer or they may view it as being slightly over-the-top.

8 Exploded means a sudden great increase – the writer uses it here to suggest that use of the written word has expanded rapidly, rather than being destroyed.

9 **a** Reference:
- 'dastardly' – caricaturing educationist, melodramatic tone
- 'silly old-fashioned thing' – patronising, colloquial

b It created a new world-wide forum for written communication that was available to everyone.

c People ignore punctuation rules in their rush to express themselves.

10 Marks on merit – answers should identify image and then make sensible comment.
- 'flits about like Tinkerbell'
- 'chases round the hillside of language like an over eager sheepdog...'
- 'muscular colon and semicolon'
- 'manly dash'

11 Humorous, self deprecating, mocking, light-hearted.

12 Answers should refer to the different meanings of the letters based on punctuation. This should be linked to the general thrust of the passage of punctuation aiding meaning and avoiding misunderstanding.

Writing

Introduction

Writing skills are a key part of the assessment requirements at Intermediate 2. They are tested whenever you write a critical essay in response to literature, and they are also specifically assessed as part of the language unit.

You may choose to write in any of the following genres: **expressive**, **creative** and **report**.

- **Expressive** covers argumentative, persuasive and reflective essays
- **Creative** includes prose fiction, drama script and poetry
- **Report** is a specialised area dealing with a single genre.

It is likely that your teacher will ask you to tackle a number of writing tasks during the session, although only one has to achieve a pass mark for the unit assessment. This will help you develop skills on a broad front and also assist your close reading skills. If you are given a choice of essay then clearly it makes sense to choose a style that you are already good at for this assignment (think back to your Standard Grade folio).

Top Tip

Be aware of the different genres in writing and think about the key features associated with each one. Make deliberate plans to include the appropriate features in your work.

Purpose of the assessment

Whatever form of essay you attempt, the assessor will be looking for evidence of your ability to express yourself in a coherent, thoughtful and logical manner. You will be expected to make full use of your vocabulary and reveal your understanding of the normal features of good writing – accurate spelling, sound sentence structures, and effective punctuation.

What you have to do

You will be required to write an essay, under controlled conditions, for internal assessment.

Four performance criteria apply to the essay:

Content

The key areas for you to consider are the **relevance** of your content to the purpose of your essay and the need for your writing to show a sound, strong development. Clearly, given that this is a National Qualification that you are attempting, some depth to your ideas is expected.

Structure

Structure refers to how you **organise** your paragraphs and ideas in your essay.

You should ensure that your paragraphs are **sequenced** properly and that you have the correct approach to the type of essay you are writing.

Expression

Expression is about **how** you say something rather than what you say.

You need to ensure at least an appropriate choice of words and a competent use of language techniques to support your content.

Technical accuracy

It will be expected that spelling, grammar and punctuation will be consistently accurate.

Some general points first:

Controlled conditions

Your teacher has to supervise your writing in such a way as to be able to verify that the work is yours. This will mean that at different points you will be asked to provide:

- a title and proposed task
- an outline plan
- a draft copy
- a final version.

For some essays your teacher may wish to see your notes, also.

Purpose

Purpose is essential for effective essay writing. Make sure you are fully aware of the style of essay you are writing and that you have a clear sense of the purpose to your writing.

Top Tip

Remember, most people find it easier to write about something they know about or have experienced. Even when you are writing creatively, make use of personal experience to help you sustain your writing.

Punctuation

If you do not punctuate properly, this will result in a failure on the grounds of technical accuracy.

One of the most common punctuation errors is the use of **comma splices**.

A comma splice occurs when, instead of putting in a **full stop** or using a **conjunction**, the writer attempts to **join together two sentences with a comma**. Just to be clear – the comma splice is a **mistake**, not a fancy way of punctuating, and its use should be avoided.

It often occurs when a pronoun is used and the writer fails to recognise that he/she has started a new sentence (action) because they are still writing about the same character or idea.

> Bryan awoke from a deep sleep, he had gone to bed very late as he had been studying hard for his English exams.

This should be written as:

> Bryan awoke from a deep sleep. He had gone to bed very late as he had been studying hard for his English exams.

Or

> Bryan awoke from a deep sleep; he had gone to bed very late as he had been studying hard for his English exams.

The semi-colon is a very useful piece of punctuation that keeps connected sentences together and helps avoid the dreaded comma splice.

Paragraphing

A paragraph is a group of sentences about the same topic. Paragraphs are the **building blocks** of a good essay.

Good paragraphs normally have good **topic sentences**. A topic sentence is a statement of the paragraph's **main idea**. Usually it opens a paragraph, although it can also act as a conclusion.

Top Tip
To become familiar with the concept of topic sentences, read through some articles and stories and see how other writers make use of them to structure their writing.

Linking your paragraphs

Paragraphs are not mini-essays. They should be linked together. Some useful transitional words and phrases that can be deployed include:

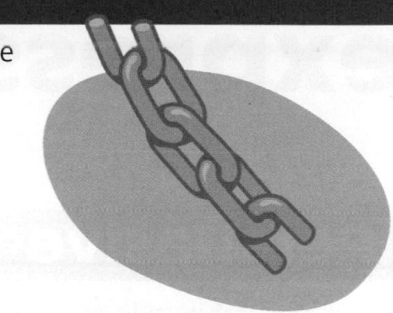

- therefore
- as a result
- nevertheless
- furthermore
- moreover
- rarely
- occasionally
- often

Try to present your ideas logically. Events, for example, should be chronological, unless you wish to create a particular effect. If you are describing a particular scene consider starting the description from a distance and then gradually get closer, thereby creating a structure to your writing.

Top Tip
Chronological refers to the normal sequence of time: morning, afternoon, evening; yesterday, today, tomorrow.

Figures of speech

Similes, **metaphors** and **personification** are techniques that will add colour and life to your writing so try to incorporate them into your work. They are explained further on page 17 of this book.

How to tackle expressive writing

Persuasive

In a persuasive style essay you are trying to convince the reader to accept your point of view on a topic. You need to make your case strongly and be able to back up your points with evidence from a variety of sources.

You should ensure that you carry out adequate research on your topic by reading articles, information leaflets, books and pamphlets and using the internet. Remember to keep a note of your sources as these must be acknowledged at the end of your essay.

In this type of essay be clear from the outset what your point of view is and state it boldly. You want to seize hold of the reader's attention and this will require a firm committed tone – for example:

> Capital punishment is a topic that is rarely far from the news.

This is reasonable opening sentence, but it could be introducing an essay in favour of capital punishment, an essay against its use, or even an essay that takes a balanced approach. Consider these alternatives:

> Capital punishment is nothing less than state sponsored murder.

> Capital punishment is the only acceptable response to the violent and criminal society we are faced with today.

In both cases the writer's stance is clear from the outset.

Having established your viewpoint in the opening paragraph, you should then build up your case with a series of paragraphs, each dealing with a different aspect of the topic.

There are a number of simple ways to develop paragraphs:

Details
Provide facts, statistics, or specific information about a topic.

Examples
Illustrate a point by giving an example.

Anecdotes
Make use of a real life experience to illustrate a point.

Comparisons
Make your point by comparing two aspects of a topic.

Contrasts
Consider opposites to highlight a topic.

Question and Answer
Pose a question and then answer it.

Once you have gathered together all your information it is time to select what you intend to use (you should have more material than you need for your essay) and then to plan out your essay.

The following general plan provides a useful format for tackling this assignment.

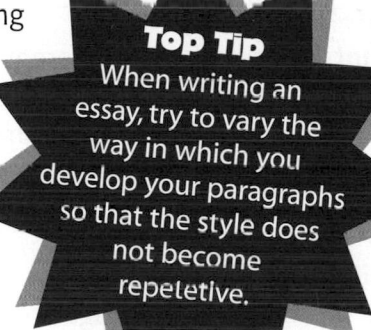

Top Tip
When writing an essay, try to vary the way in which you develop your paragraphs so that the style does not become repetetive.

Paragraph 1
Statement of attitude – state your topic and make clear your stance.

Paragraph 2
Argument 1 – make the first points in support of your position and then develop the paragraph through one of the techniques suggested.

Paragraph 3
Argument 2 – make your second point, and then develop it, using a different technique to paragraph 1.

Paragraph 4
Argument 3 – again, make your point, and then develop it, using a different technique from the previous paragraphs.

Paragraph 5
Deal with opposite viewpoint – here you should introduce an argument that might be used against your viewpoint and answer it (what you are doing here is demonstrating confidence in your own position by taking account of other points of view).

Paragraph 6
Restatement of attitude – finish by strongly restating your opening point of view, drawing on some of your arguments to underline your position.

Argumentative

In an argumentative essay you will deal with at least two different viewpoints and your line of argument will explore the issue and the varying points of view.

The approach is not dissimilar to that for a persuasive essay. The following plan is a useful structure:

Paragraph 1

Introduce your subject and indicate some of the main issues you intend to discuss.

Paragraph 2

Viewpoint A – introduce an aspect relating to the subject and then outline the main argument that might be used to support it and comment on/evaluate the issue.

Paragraph 3

Viewpoint A – introduce a second aspect relating to the subject, again outline the main argument that might be used to support it and comment on/evaluate the issue.

Paragraph 4

Viewpoint B – introduce a different approach to the subject, and then outline the main argument that might be used to support this view and comment on/evaluate the issue.

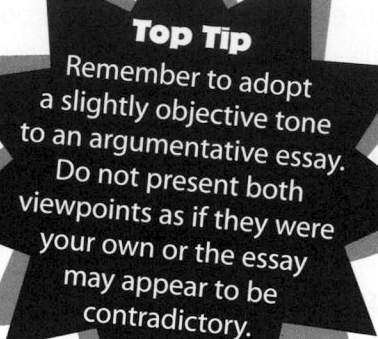

Top Tip
Remember to adopt a slightly objective tone to an argumentative essay. Do not present both viewpoints as if they were your own or the essay may appear to be contradictory.

Paragraph 5

Viewpoint B – introduce a further aspect of the subject from the second viewpoint, again outline the main argument that might be used to support it and comment on/evaluate the issue.

Paragraph 6

Compare the contrary viewpoints and try to balance the weight of evidence used to support the differing views. Arrive at a **conclusion**, which does not necessarily need to be in favour of either side of the argument.

Reflective

This is a popular essay format and it has the benefit of being based on your own experiences. You will almost certainly have tackled essays such as this at Standard Grade. **However, while an element of story telling is acceptable at Standard Grade, for your Intermediate 2 essay you should avoid simply retelling the story of a particular event.**

That is why this essay is referred to as a **'reflective'** rather than a **'personal experience'** task – to emphasise the importance of actually thinking about and commenting on the experience. You are trying to demonstrate the insight you have gained from the event.

Try to express your thoughts and feelings as clearly as you can and show how the experience has had an impact on you. Convey to the reader a clear sense of your own personal involvement and reveal any understanding that has developed on your part as a result of the event being discussed.

Write sensitively about yourself, allowing your personality to shine through. Make full use of well-chosen words and where appropriate figurative language such as similes and metaphors. Sometimes reflective essays can be a bit melodramatic and clichéd – try to avoid this.

Be careful not to allow the detail of an event to overwhelm the writing. A good essay will concentrate on your thoughts, feelings and reactions.

Clichés are overused phrases that have lost their ability to have any real impact on the reader – 'a shiver ran down my spine'; 'he was like a bull in a china shop'. **Avoid using them.**

Consider the following opening paragraphs, which attempt to create the 'feel' of a reflective essay:

> *Looking back, I sometimes wonder how those around me ever managed to put up with my mood swings. One moment I would be on a high and charging forward and then the next there wasn't a shade of blue deep enough for my depression ...*

> *Pondering the future can be difficult when you are only sixteen – there are just so many possibilities that it is difficult to be certain about anything. One thing I am clear about however is that changes are most definitely on the way ...*

> *It was a difficult time for everyone and the experience has certainly left its mark on me. I see so many things differently as a result of dealing with that situation and I suppose I have grown up in a number of important ways. I had to really ...*

Top Tip
Avoid excessive narrative in a reflective essay. Concentrate on your thoughts and feelings; your personal reaction.

How to tackle creative writing

Introduction

Creative writing covers **poetry**, **drama** and **prose**. For many candidates a short story will be the preferred option although within the prose genre a wide range of options is available including areas such as a diary / journal, the opening chapter of a novel and for some candidates the option of either poetry or drama may be particularly appropriate.

Language

Your word choice in creative writing is vital. Pick words that create vivid, vibrant pictures or that convey feelings and emotions with precision and accuracy. Dull, pedestrian word-choice will create dull pedestrian writing.

Examples

Verb: 'No' he **said**. Why use a dull simple word like '**said**'?

Alternatives: whispered, croaked, screamed, rasped, shouted, exclaimed, cried, whimpered, confided, retorted, snapped, laughed … all of these add descriptive detail.

Adjective: Adjectives are words that **describe** a noun. They improve your writing by enhancing its descriptive qualities:

> The tree stood alone.
> The leafless tree stood alone.
> The small, leafless, lifeless tree stood alone.
>
> The tree stood alone.
> The tall tree stood alone.
> The tall, proud tree stood alone.

Your choice of adjectives can have quite an impact on the meaning and tone of your writing.

Active voice

Using what is referred to as the active voice can make your verbs more effective – giving a greater sense of directness to your writing.

Keri drove her new car with a mixture of fear and bravado.

As opposed to the passive voice:

The new car was driven by Keri with a mixture of fear and bravado.

Syntax – improving sentence structure

Candidates often let themselves down by using a repetitive, pedestrian style in relation to their sentence structures.

Sentences are normally formed around a **verb**, which is a word or phrase describing the **action**, and the verb will have a subject (the person or thing doing whatever is being done). The usual sentence structure will have the subject coming first, followed by the verb, and then followed by any additional information being provided.

In Close Reading you are often asked to comment on the **syntax** of a sentence, where the writer has altered the normal word order to create a particular effect, perhaps beginning with an adverb to create a particular effect such as emphasising how something was done. For example:

> Quietly, the teacher crept up on the pupil whose head was resting peacefully on his desk.

You should attempt to do the same in your own writing.

Joining sentences

Normally when we join two sentences together we often use a conjunction:

> Keri sat on the settee. She began to read the novel she had chosen for her 'Personal Study'.

becomes

> Keri sat on the settee and began to read the novel she had chosen for her 'Personal Study'.

Another way of achieving this, however, is to take one of the verbs and to turn it into the '–ing' (present participle) form and then to use it as the opening of the sentence:

> Sitting on the settee, Keri began to read the novel she had chosen for her 'Personal Study'.

Varying our sentence structures, like this, improves our writing. In this case we have the bonus of starting the sentence with a verb, which creates a sense of action.

This structure also allows us to build up a complex sentence without overusing conjunctions such as 'and'.

> Sitting on the settee, Keri began to read the novel she had chosen for her 'Personal Study' and almost at once she became hooked by its exciting storyline.

A note of caution!

If you are using this technique make sure that the subject of both verbs is the same, otherwise you may end up writing nonsense!

Arriving home from ice-hockey practice, Bryan immediately headed for a warm soak in a freshly run bath.

Correct – because Bryan is arriving home and Bryan heads for a warm soak.

However, if the subjects are different we cannot make a sensible sentence.

The referee blew the whistle. The striker shot and scored the penalty.

Blowing the whistle, the striker shot and scored the penalty.

This would mean that the striker blew the whistle and then scored a goal.

In this case if we wished to join the sentences we would use a conjunction (linking word/connective)

After the referee blew the whistle, the striker shot and scored the penalty.

Top Tip
Varying your sentence structures reveals your skill with language and helps to create a more interesting piece of writing.

Writing a short story

Three elements

A short story should have **three** elements:

- **character**
- **setting**
- **plot**.

Character

In a short story you should limit yourself to one or two central characters, only. Try to create a personality for your character. You can do this by describing the way he/she behaves; having other characters talk about the person; through the things your character does or thinks.

Using direct speech can bring your characters to life!

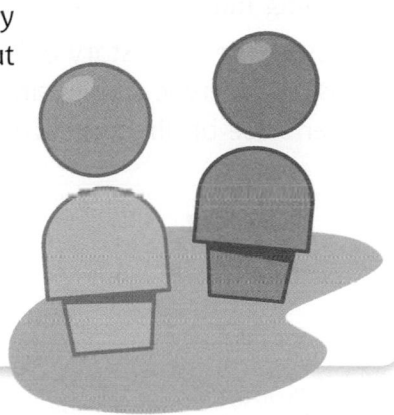

> 'I was really scared, Sir. Terrified in fact. It was probably the worst moment of my entire life!'
>
> 'Don't worry about it – everyone feels like that after an English exam,' replied the teacher, kindly.

Setting

Setting is also important for your story. Think about where and when your story takes place. You will find it easier if the setting is reasonably familiar to you rather than something too fantastical. Think also about the atmosphere and mood that you wish to create and choose descriptive words that build up an effective setting.

It's always useful to think in terms of your five senses when trying create mood and atmosphere:

- sight
- sound
- smell
- taste
- touch.

Plot

A plot has three stages: **beginning** – **middle** – **end**. These are not equal stages in terms of length, however.

The **beginning** is where you set the scene and introduce the key characters. The **middle** section builds the storyline towards its turning point and the **end** is where matters are resolved.

Good stories involve **change**. At the conclusion of your story someone or something has to be different – otherwise you haven't really told a story, simply described a situation. The change does not have to be monumental but it should allow the reader to share in the experience – for example, a character may discover that he/she has more courage than they thought or that they cared more about something than they had realised.

A story without change is like saying to someone, 'Wait till I tell you what happened!' And then when you are eagerly pressed for details, you reply, 'Nothing much.'

Consider the short story below, written by a pupil who was asked to create a ghost/horror type story, using a setting that was familiar. Think about the writer's use of direct speech, descriptive language and simplicity of plot.

Learning!

"Lee?"

"Here."

"Shaun?"

"Here."

"Robert?"

"Are ye blind? I'm sitting right in front of you!" The class giggled. Mr. Venge lifted his head with a weary sigh.

"Just answer your name, please. I don't have time for your usual carry-on, Robert," he intoned. He had tried so hard to like his pupils and to have them like him. But everything he had done for them had been hurled back in his face. Now he was just too tired to try anymore.

"Ooh, sorree," replied the malevolent child perched on the edge of his seat. "I thought that wis your joab – to hiv time for us poor weans. If yer too tired maybe ye should get to yir bed earlier. Whit time did ye go to bed, sir?"

"Listen Robert, I've had just about as much as I'm prepared to take from you. Be quiet and don't annoy me or you'll be sorry, very sorry!"

"Ooh, I'm scared, Sir," he replied, whilst the rest of the jeering pack responded to the bell by knocking over chairs and desks on their way out of the room. Mr. Venge watched then go and then sunk his head into his hands. This had to stop. His life wasn't worth living. Things couldn't go on.

That night he left the school with his coat pulled tightly around him. Rain rattled off the ground and an icy wind plucked at his face.

"Goodnight baldy!" jeered a voice from the group of pupils loitering at the gate. He spied Robert's grinning face and then hurried on his way. Darkness soon cloaked him from the sight of the group but the sound of their laughter haunted him as he quietly slipped in behind a sprawling hawthorn bush. He waited ...

"Lee?"

"Here."

"Shaun?"

"Here."

"Robert?"

Silence.

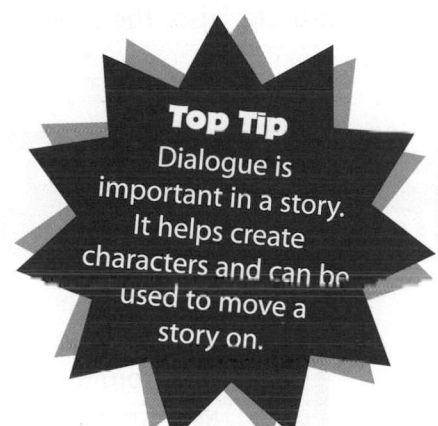

Top Tip
Dialogue is important in a story. It helps create characters and can be used to move a story on.

"No one know where Robert is?"

Still, silence.

"No, no one knows where Robert is," said the teacher, and this time it wasn't a question. His steely voice rang across the classroom with the finality of a prison gate slamming closed.

That evening, as he made his way home, he passed by a group of pupils huddled close together at the school entrance. The Police had been questioning everyone about Robert's disappearance. As he approached, Mr Venge looked up. "Good night children," he hissed. "So sorree to hear that Robert is missing. Probably all a mistake. Still, we live and learn eh? Well, some of us do." His eyes glinted at them. "See you in the morning." Then he added, "You hope ..."

The sound of his laughter echoed back to the group as he faded into the evening mist that swirled around the dismal streets.

"Goodnight, Mr. Venge, Sir," they chorused in a uniform voice, but he had already turned the corner and darkness had swallowed him up.

Writing a report

Introduction

Report writing differs from argumentative/persuasive writing in that you are attempting to present **complex** information in a **non-personal**, **objective** fashion.

Step 1 – establish remit

With your teacher, agree the topic and focus of your planned report. This should be summarised in a short statement of the report's purpose. Your statement should indicate, also, the intended sources of information.

Step 2 – gather and organise information

Gather and collate key information from your sources. The minimum number of sources must be four, and these can be from a wide range of categories such as articles, surveys, maps, television, databases and so on.

In terms of **collating** information a few simple steps apply:

Use your task to **plan** your notes. For example, imagine you have chosen to write a report on sectarianism in Scottish society. To focus your task you might decide to firstly define the nature of sectarianism; to consider the extent of its presence in Scottish society and the damage it does; and finally to outline any initiatives that have been launched to tackle the problem. (Your essay requires to have a logical structure to it, whatever topic you choose.)

Each of these areas will help you **organise** information into different sections of your report. Write each at the head of a separate piece of paper. Then read through your sources.

As you read through the sources highlight or note the **key points** made and list them under the appropriate heading from your task. Try to put the points into your own words at this stage as this will help you avoid copying in your final essay.

Likely **sources** for this essay might include a Scottish Executive press release on tackling sectarianism; statements from Celtic and Rangers football clubs on their policy against sectarianism; a newspaper clipping about a sectarian incident, with quotations from the victim; statistics on crimes with sectarian connections; a policy document from an Education Authority.

Once you have made your notes you need to reorganise the information you have gathered as it will be in the random order that you read the sources. Look to see the connections between different items of information as this will help you create cohesive paragraphs when you start writing.

Step 3 – write the report

Write your report in **formal prose**. This means that you should avoid shortcuts such as contracting words (**Don't!**); that you **do not use** quotations or colloquialisms; and that you avoid using figurative or flowery language.

Reports tend to be written in the **present tense** – so do this.

Present the information as you have found it and try to keep your own personal opinion out of the essay. The primary purpose of your report is to **inform** the reader – not to persuade him or her, although you are allowed to draw a conclusion based on the information you have presented.

You may use **diagrams**, **charts** and **graphs** in your report if they are required by the topic. You may use headings and bullet points, also, to organise information. (This can be particularly useful if your report is based upon work you are doing in a different subject.)

A few tips to remember

- Where you come across statistics, concentrate on the point being made in the information rather than the bald figures.

- Anecdotes (personal experiences/stories) are useful to illustrate an aspect of a situation, but it is the point that is being made that you should concentrate on for your notes, not the details of the story.

- Similarly, when you are given a list of examples, focus on what they are examples of rather than the examples themselves.

- Just because something is in a newspaper or on the internet doesn't mean that it is true – try to verify your sources.

Top Tip

A report for English can be drawn from work you carry out in a different subject, for example Religious and Moral Education or History/Geography. However, the requirements for passing are the same, and if you wish to pursue this path you would need to get the agreement of your teacher, who would have to be satisfied that the work was essentially your own.

Textual analysis

Introduction

Textual analysis is about you responding **critically** to an unseen piece of literature. You will be assessed by being asked specific questions on a short text – which can be a poem, a prose extract, or a drama extract.

The unit test in Literature requires a NAB pass in Textual analysis.

Purpose of the assessment

Textual analysis, as with the critical essay, is concerned with your ability to **respond thoughtfully** to a literary text. The NAB assessment will test your ability to understand the writer's purpose, to appreciate the writer's craft, and to demonstrate a genuinely personal response to the text.

What you have to do

You will be asked a set of questions on a given text or extract. These will test the following areas:

Understanding

These questions will test your ability to demonstrate understanding of the **main concerns** and **significant details** of the text.

Analysis

These questions test your ability to **examine** and **explain** how aspects of **structure**, **language** and **style** help convey meaning and create impact.

Evaluation

These questions test your ability to demonstrate a degree of **personal response** to the ideas in the text and assess the effectiveness of the writer in conveying a view or experience.

How to tackle textual analysis

Be clear about the type of question being asked as this will help ensure that your answer is relevant.

- **Understanding** style questions are about what is being said by the writer.
- **Analysis** style questions are about how it is being said.
- **Evaluation** style questions are about how well it is being done.

'what' = Understanding   'how' = Analysis   'to what extent'/'how well' = Evaluation

Consider the following short poem by Alfred Lord Tennyson and the practice questions that follow.

The Eagle

He clasps the crag with hooked hands;
Close to the sun in lonely lands,
Ringed with the azure world, he stands.

The wrinkled sea beneath him crawls;
He watches from his mountain walls,
And like a thunderbolt he falls.
(Azure = sky-blue)

As you read the poem it is helpful to highlight language features and images as they strike you. So the above poem might look something like this:

The Eagle

He clasps the crag with **hooked** **hands**;	highlight the use of alliteration
Close to the sun in **(lonely lands)**,	brackets for strong image
Ringed with the azure world, **he stands**.	comma used to separate out the end phrase
The **wrinkled** sea beneath him **crawls**;	metaphor/effective word choice
He watches from **his mountain walls**,	sense of ownership
And **like a thunderbolt he falls**.	simile

Some textual questions might be:

Q What impression of the eagle is created in stanza one? (An understanding question)

A *That of a strong, superior creature.*

Q How does the poet create this impression? (An analysis question)

A *Reference could be made to word choice:*
'clasps' = sense of power and strength
'Close to the sun' = high up. Looking down on everything else.
'lonely lands' = creates sense of isolation, singularity of eagle
'he stands' = comma before this phrase isolates it, underlines the way the eagle appears to be apart, aloof.

Q How does the poet suggest that the eagle is like a ruler, in the opening line of stanza 2? (An analysis question)

A *He refers to the waves' 'wrinkles', crawling beneath him as if they were like servants bowing before their master or King.*

Q How effective is the last line of the poem? (An evaluation question.)

A *It is very effective. The simile used suggests the eagle diving down on its prey 'like a thunderbolt' suggesting that it is powerful and unexpected like part of a storm.*

Top Tip

In responding to textual analysis questions you should attempt to use the correct terminology for particular aspects of language such as the use of similes and metaphors. A guide to technical terms is included in Appendix A (see page 88).

Textual analysis practice

Practice papers

Try the practice papers that follow and then work through the guided marking scheme, attempting to learn from any mistakes that you make.

Practice A

In this poem by Margaret Taylor, a woman walks home alone on a dismal wet evening. Her sense of loneliness is reflected in her surroundings.

Loneliness

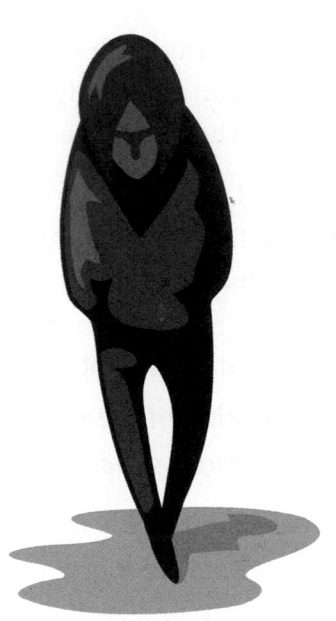

1   Nightmare town,
    The streets silent, dark
    Sabbath empty
    Follow me home:
5   I walk slowly
    And the rain-wet stones
    Wink under the sodium flares,
    I hear them snigger
    As I bend my head to the rain:
10 I must have walked this road
    This endless road
    A thousand years,
    Yet I never meet a soul,
    Even the paper scraps
15 Draw themselves aside,
    The houses draw up,
    From their dank gardens,
    But their prim laces never stir –
    Oh God is there no one in this town?

Margaret Taylor

Questions – Practice A

1 What impression is created by the opening words of the poem?   2

2 Consider lines 2-4.
How does the poet convey the woman's feelings as she walks home?   2

3 Why might the woman 'walk slowly'?   1

4 Consider lines 6-8.
The poet is trying to capture the woman's sense of vulnerability. How effective
do you find the imagery used in these lines?   4

5 The woman 'bend(s)' (line 9) her head to avoid the rain being blown into her face.
What other reason might there be for her bending her head?   1

6 Consider lines 10-12.
    a Identify the techniques used by the writer to suggest the long-term nature
       of the woman's loneliness.   2
    b How does the poet's use of punctuation help support the meaning of
       these lines?   1
    c The journey might be said to be a metaphor for the woman's life.
       What does this statement mean?   2

7 Comment on the writer's use of the word 'soul' (line 13) rather than a more literal
word such as person.   1

8 Consider lines 14-18.
How do these lines emphasise the woman's sense of rejection?   2

9 The last line has a different tone from the rest of the poem.
How effective do you find this as a conclusion to the poem?   2

Total = 20 marks

Practice B

Read the following extract from the play *Bold Girls*, by Rhona Munro. In this scene two friends are talking after a night out. Michael is the dead husband of one of the friends, Marie. His photograph hangs on the wall.

Marie: See Cassie, I've had better times with Michael than a lot of women get in their whole lives with a man.

Cassie: And that's what keeps you going?

5   **Marie:** It's a warming kind of thought.

Cassie holds out her arms to Michael's pictures

Cassie: (singing) "Thanks – for the memories."

Marie: Oh Cassie.

Cassie: That doesn't work, Marie. I've tried to keep myself warm
10   that way. Find some man with good hands and a warm skin and wrap him round you to keep the rain off; you'll be damp in the end anyway.

Marie: Cassie, don't talk like that; you know you've not done half the wild things you make out.

Cassie: Not a quarter of what I wanted to Marie, but enough to know
15   it doesn't work. Grabbing onto some man because he smells like excitement, he smells like escape. They can't take you anywhere except the back seat of their car. They're all the same.

Marie: If that's what you think of them that's all you'll find.

Cassie gets up to stand, looking at Michael.

20   **Cassie:** They are *all* the same, Marie.

Marie: No.

Cassie: *No*, not *Michael*. (*Sarcastically*) Wasn't he just the perfect man, the perfect saint of a man.

Marie: He was no saint.

25   **Cassie:** He was not.

Marie: I never said he was a saint.

Cassie: Not much perfect about him.

Marie: We cared for each other! We were honest with each other.

Cassie: Honest!?

30   **Marie:** We were. He was a good man.

Cassie: Good!? He was a lying worm like every one of them.

There is a pause

Marie: I think you should go home, Cassie.

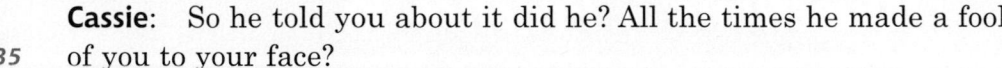

Cassie: So he told you about it did he? All the times he made a fool
35   of you to your face?

Marie: Just go now.

Cassie: I don't believe you could have kept that smile on your face
Marie, not if he was honestly telling you what he was up to.

Marie: Cassie…

40   **Cassie:**   Making a fool of you with all those women.

There is a pause

Marie: I heard the stories. Of course I heard them.

Cassie: Did you though?

Marie: He was a great-looking man. He was away a lot. There were
45   bound to be stories.

Cassie: There were books of them, Marie.

Marie: But if there'd been any truth in them Michael would have
told me himself.

Cassie: Oh *Marie!*

50   **Marie:**   That's trust, Cassie.

Cassie: That's *stupidity*, Marie. You haven't the sense of a hen with
its head off!

Marie: Michael would no more lie to me than you would, Cassie.

Cassie: Well we both did! That's what I'm telling you Marie! We were
55   both lying to you for years!

Marie freezes where she is.

Questions – Practice B

1 Why has the writer used inverted commas around the words
"Thanks – for the memories" (line 7)?   1

2 Consider lines 1-13.
  a What initial impression do you get of Cassie?   1
  b How is this created by the writer?   3

3 'He smells like excitement, he smells like escape' (lines 15-16)
Comment on the writer's choice of language here   2

4 'They are *all* the same' (line 20).
  a Why is the word 'all' in italics here?   1
  b How does the stage direction support this purpose?   1

5 How does the writer build a sense of tension as the conversation continues?   4

6 Explain the different impact achieved by each of the dramatic pauses
(line 32 and line 41).   4

7 'Michael would have told me himself' (lines 47-48)
How does Cassie feel about Marie's statement?   2

8 'Marie: That's trust, Cassie
Cassie: That's stupidity, Marie...' (lines 50-51)
How effectively does this exchange illustrate the contrast between the
two characters?   2

9 What is the full impact and meaning of Cassie's final speech (lines 54-55)?   4

Total = 25 marks

Practice C

In this extract from *Touching the Void*, the writer, Joe Simpson, sets the scene for the true-life story of a mountain climb that goes disastrously wrong.

Beneath the Mountain Lakes

I was lying in my sleeping bag, staring at the light filtering through the red and green fabric of the dome tent. Simon was snoring loudly, occasionally twitching in his dream world. We could have been anywhere.

5 There is a peculiar anonymity about being in tents. Once the zip is closed and the outside world barred from sight, all sense of location disappears. Scotland, the French Alps, the Karakorum, it was always the same. The sounds of rustling, of fabric flapping in the

10 wind, or of rainfall, the feel of hard lumps under the ground sheet, the smells of rancid socks and sweat – these are the universals, as comforting as the warmth of the down sleeping bag.

Outside, in a lightening sky, the peaks would be catching the first of the morning sun, with perhaps even a condor cresting the thermals

15 above the tent. That wasn't too fanciful either since I had seen one circling the camp the previous afternoon. We were in the middle of the Cordillera Huayhuash, in the Peruvian Andes, separated from the nearest village by twenty-eight miles of rough walking, and surrounded by the most spectacular ring of ice mountains I had ever

20 seen, and the only indication of this from within our tent was the regular roaring of avalanches falling off Cerro Sarapo.

I felt a homely affection for the warm security of the tent, and reluctantly wormed out of my bag to face the prospect of lighting the stove. It had snowed a little during the night, and the grass crunched

25 frostily under my feet as I padded over to the cooking rock. There was no sign of Richard stirring as I passed his tiny one-man tent, half collapsed and whitened with hoar frost.

Squatting under the lee of the overhanging rock that had become our kitchen, I relished this moment when I could be entirely alone. I

30 fiddled with the petrol stove which was mulishly objecting to both the temperature and the rusty petrol with which I had filled it. I resorted to brutal coercion when coaxing failed and sat it atop a propane gas stove going full blast. It burst into vigorous life, spluttering out two-foot-high flames in petulant revolt against the dirty petrol.

35 As the pan of water slowly heated, I looked around at the wide, dry and rock-strewn river bed, the erratic boulder under which I crouched marking the site at a distance in all but the worst weather. A huge, almost vertical wall of ice and snow soared upwards to the summit of Cerro Sarapo directly in front of the camp, no more than a mile and a

40 half away. Rising from the sea of moraine to my left, two spectacular and extravagant castles of sugar icing, Yerupaja and Rasac,

dominated the camp site. The majestic 21,000-foot Siula Grande lay behind Sarapo and was not visible. It had been climbed for the first time in 1936 by two bold Germans via the North Ridge. There had

45   been few ascents since then, and the true prize, the daunting 4,500-feet West Face had so far defeated all attempts.

I turned off the stove and gingerly slopped the water into three large mugs. The sun hadn't cleared the ridge of the mountains opposite and it was still chilly in the shadows.

50   'There's a brew ready, if you're still alive in there,' I announced cheerfully.

from Touching the Void by Joe Simpson, published by Jonathan Cape. *Reprinted by permission of The Random House Group.*

Questions – Practice C

1 Consider lines 1-12.
  a What does the writer mean by 'a peculiar anonymity' (line 5)? **2**
  b How does the structure of the last sentence in paragraph one (lines 9-12), develop this meaning? **2**

2 Consider lines 13-21.
  a What impression is created by the writer's reference to 'even a condor cresting the thermals above the tent' (lines 14-15)? **1**
  b How does the writer create a sense of isolation about the camp site? **2**
  c 'regular roaring of avalanches' (line 21).
     How effective is this metaphor in developing a sense of the location? **2**

3 Consider lines 22-27.
  a 'I felt a homely affection for the warm security of the tent' (line 22).
     Explain what is meant by this expression. **2**
  b How does the writer's word choice in the remainder of this sentence continue this same sentiment? **1**
  c Choose one example of descriptive detail from the remainder of the paragraph and show how it contrasts with the atmosphere of the opening sentence. **2**

4 Consider lines 28-34.
  a 'I relished this moment when I could be entirely alone.'
     How does the writer's word choice convey his pleasure at this point? **1**
  b Why do you think he feels this way? **1**
  c By examining the writer's word choice, show how he creates the impression of a struggle between himself and the stove. **4**

5 Consider lines 35-46.
  a What clue is given in lines 35-37 as to why they may have chosen this particular site? **1**
  b Choose two expressions from lines 37-46 that help you understand the scale and splendour of the mountains surrounding the camp-site and explain why you have chosen them. **4**
  c How does the writer make clear in lines 43-46, the difficulties involved in climbing the Siula Grande? **3**

6 Consider lines 47-51.
  Why do you think the writer feels cheerful? **2**

Total = 30 marks

Answers – Practice A

1   *Answers should pick up on the use of the word 'nightmare' to suggest sense of fear, being frightened, unpleasant, etc.*

2   *Sense of being followed/stalked; isolation emphasised by word choice: 'silent', 'Sabbath empty'; echo of nightmare reference in the use of the word 'dark'.*

3   *Attempt to reassure herself; result of her fear.*

4   *Answers should deal with the idea of the woman being the victim of a conspiracy, nasty joke.*
Possible references:
- *'wink' – literally the lights lashing off the wet ground but connotation of a prank being played behind someone's back*
- *'snigger – literally the sound of the rain hitting off the ground but connotation of a sly, malevolent laugh.*

5   *Weighed down by her loneliness; senses of submission, giving-up.*

6   **a** *repetition – 'I must have walked this road this endless road'*
      hyperbole – 'a thousand years'
      word choice – 'endless'
  b *Absence of punctuation causes lines to run through into each other, echoing the idea of 'endless'.*
  c *The road as well as being a physical journey is also her journey though life and she feels that her loneliness is as never ending as the road she is walking on.*

7   *Person would simply imply a physical presence, whereas 'soul' suggest some human connection, like a 'soul-mate'.*

8   *Idea of rubbish in the street, which is being blown by the wind, turning away from her; coupled with the people inside the houses showing no interest as they don't even look out to see who is passing.*

9   *Separated out by a dash. Tone is like a spoken plea, cry of desperation. Effective because it is as if all the poet's feelings have built up and then burst out in a cry for help.*

Answers – Practice B

1   The words are a lyric from a song so they are being quoted.
Accept either aspect for a mark.

2   **a**   That she is a bit sarcastic/cheeky/abrasive.
   b   Possible references:
   - querying tone of 'And that's what keeps you going?'
   - stage direction of arms out, singing to the picture of Michael, mocking stance
   - dismissive tone of 'you'll be damp in the end anyway'
   - Marie's reference to Cassie's claim to wild behaviour.

3   Concentration on sense of smell, 'excitement' suggests action/interest in her life, 'escape' implies her dissatisfaction with her life as it is.

4   **a**   To emphasise Cassie's inclusion of Michael in her reference.
   b   She stands looking at his picture.

5   Possible references:
   - Marie's abrupt one word rejection of Cassie's statement, 'No.'
   - Cassie's sarcastic response and emphasis on naming Michael
   - The combative nature of the dialogue with Marie defending Michael and Cassie needling about him.
   - Cassie's outburst of 'Honest' and the questioning tone.
   - Cassie's insult about Michael being a 'lying worm'.

6   After the first pause, line 32, Marie is staying calm and sending her friend home to finish the argument. She doesn't want to hear any more. After the second pause she gives in to Cassie's argument and tries to respond to her claims.

7   She feels saddened/surprised by Marie's naïve belief that Michael would have told her the truth.

8   Effective. Marie seems to be more mild-mannered and trusting whereas Cassie is outspoken and streetwise.

9   Some points on impact and meaning are as follows:
   - It reveals that Cassie and Michael had an affair that they both covered up and kept hidden from Marie.
   - Marie's trust in Michael is shown to be unfounded.
   - Cassie's earlier comments are seen to be based on experience rather than just being a prejudice.
   - Marie is stunned by the revelation and she 'freezes' so clearly the friendship between the two women is under pressure.

Answers – Practice C

1 **a** *Strange sense of being unspecific/lacking exact location, etc.*

    b *The writer uses a dash to separate out a list of details that are constant to being in a tent anywhere, which he refers as the 'universals', suggesting that these are the hallmarks of being under canvas.*

2 **a** *Visual image a single bird circling in the sky – accept idea a being alone, being high in the mountains, being at one with nature, etc.*

    b *Makes reference to the distance from the nearest village and the difficulty of travelling between the two spots/use of the words 'surrounded by ... ring of ice mountains' as if they are almost cut off from civilisation.*

    c *'roaring' echoes the idea of wilderness and sense of nature's power. Reference to frequent avalanches hints at potential danger and the remoteness of the location.*

3 **a** *It is as if the tent is their home, offering sense of comfort and protection.*

    b *His reluctance to leave the warmth of his sleeping bag is conveyed by the use of the word 'wormed' as if he had been cocooned tight in its warmth and he has to wriggle his way out.*

    c *Possible references:*
- *'crunched frostily' – onomatopoeiac quality of phrase suggesting the sharp coldness outside the tent*
- *'whitened with hoar frost' – visual image of the outside coldness, contrasting with the internal warmth.*

4 **a** *'relished' suggests taking great pleasure in something*

    b *Possible answers might be that he could appreciate the splendour around him more fully, that as he is sharing a small tent he feels more relaxed on his own, that it gives him some privacy*

    c *References (any two fully explained for full marks):*
- *'Mulishly objecting': metaphorical, sense of stubborn refusal to cooperate*
- *'Brutal coercion': physical force being used*
- *'Coaxing failed': gentle persuasion unsuccessful*
- *'Petulant revolt': sullen rebellion.*

5 **a** *The reference to the rock being visible unless it was really bad weather suggest that it may have been chosen as it would be easy to find/spot, etc.*

    b *'a huge, almost vertical wall of ice and snow soared upwards to the summit'*
Suggestion of scale in the word 'huge'/'vertical wall of ice and snow' image of sheer domination of the snow face/'soared upwards' – soared suggests power, speed and scale; alliterative link with summit, idea of pinnacle.

'Two spectacular and extravagant castles of sugar icing'
'spectacular' suggesting visual splendour/'extravagant' suggesting
opulence and scale of the mountains/'sugar icing' unusual image
suggesting the prettiness of the scene or the apparent delicacy of
the snow formations.

c *Use of the word 'bold' to describe the German climbers suggesting*
that they were brave, implying the danger involved in the climb.
Reference to the limited number of successful climbs since 1936
suggesting that it was not an easy task.
Use of the word 'daunting' which means intimidating to make clear
that such a climb would be difficult.
Reference to the fact that no-one had been successful in climbing
the West face yet – 'defeated all attempts'.

6 *He is enjoying the experience looking forward to the challenge of the*
climb/has woken up fully – accept any sensible answer based on content
of passage.

Critical essay

Introduction

In the examination you will need to write two critical essays in response to unseen tasks. You should consider your Personal Study unit as a critical essay, also, and this is a required unit pass, although for that assessment you will create your own task.

The skills required for both assessments are essentially the same and they build upon the work you did at Standard Grade for your reading folio, where most candidates submit three critical essays. A key difference is that you do not get to re-draft work, so the skills involved have to become second-nature to you, in order that you can complete tasks in the specified time allowed (another key difference from Standard Grade).

Purpose of the assessment

A critical essay assessment is designed to test your ability to respond thoughtfully to a literary text, be it a poem, a play, a novel or a short story. The marker wishes to know if you have understood the writer's purpose, if you can comment effectively on the writer's use of literary technique, and if you can demonstrate a genuine personal response to the text.

In the examination you must respond to the actual task set. This lets the marker see that you are not simply regurgitating a set of notes that you have learned off by rote but are actually able to apply your knowledge and understanding of the text in a focused manner.

To gain knowledge and understanding you will study a number of texts in class and your teacher will direct you towards key features through class work and discussion. It is important, however, that you take personal responsibility for applying yourself to such study, in order to maximise your learning, and for constantly revising texts as your examination approaches.

Top Tip
Literary texts should be revisited as often as possible over the course of a session. A text finished before Christmas will not be fresh in your mind by May without it being re-read.

What you have to do

You will be asked to write two essays in the exam, each from a different genre. The genres used in the examination paper are drama, prose (which includes fiction and non-fiction), poetry, mass media and language. These last two should only be tackled if you have prepared for them during your course. Most schools concentrate on the first three areas.

Specifically, you are required to show competence in the following areas:

Understanding

Demonstrate, as required by the task set, your understanding of the **key aspects** and main issues of the text(s) studied. To do this you will need to **identify significant sections** in the text(s). Understanding is about responding to the key theme of the text(s) and not about being able to re-tell the story.

Analysis

Explain ways in which aspects of the writing such as **narrative stance**, **characterisation**, **language** and **structure** contribute to the meaning and effect of the text. To do this you will need to make relevant quotations or refer to appropriate incidents/details in the text in order to support any comments you make.

Evaluation

Say what you thought about the text and how well you feel the **writer** has **conveyed** or **explored** a particular viewpoint. The key point in making an evaluation is to justify what you are saying by reference to the text.

Expression

This area is about assessing your **writing skills**: **word choice**, **sentencing**, **punctuation** and **paragraphing** are all important. How well have you conveyed your **point of view**? Is your essay **well-organised**? Have you responded clearly to the task by presenting a **clear line of thought** in your argument? Have you used **critical terminology** correctly, e.g. reference to characterisation; setting; the use of rhyme (see Appendix A, page 88)?

Top Tip

The performance criteria should not be seen as a checklist as a good critical essay creates an overall impression on the marker as a result of these different areas interacting. However, each area needs to be present in order to achieve a pass.

How to tackle critical essay writing

Introduction

The texts you read will be of a high quality, chosen by your teacher because he/she thinks that they have something valid to communicate to the reader. The key difference between quality literary texts and general run-of-the mill fiction is that good texts have something to say to the reader about the human condition; they are not simply to entertain the reader, although they do that as well.

Your aim in your essay is to show the marker that you have understood the writer's message/concern, and to demonstrate your response to it.

Focus on the task

Re-telling the storyline of a text does not create a good essay. Answers that rely heavily on 'narrative content' are likely to fail. A general review type answer is unlikely to achieve a pass, also. You must respond to the question set – a key reason for failure in the exam is the inability of the candidate to actually respond to the task set in the question.

You must focus on the assignment and respond to its detail. This is what allows you to demonstrate your understanding of the key elements, central concerns and significant details of the text(s).

Many answers have clearly been prepared before the exam and then they are twisted in some way in an attempt to fit the question but invariably such essays achieve a poor mark because of their lack of relevance. 'Topping and tailing' (sticking in a reference to the task in the first and last paragraph and then filling the rest of the essay with a pre-learned response) is a common feature of essays that score badly. **If you wish to pass, do not adopt this approach.**

Planning your essay

To ensure that you focus on the task, create a title for your essay based on the detail of the question. This will set up the required response. Your title is a working title, part of your planning. It does not form part of your answer and it does not have to be catchy or clever. To create a good title, take the words of the question and refocus them.

An effective method of planning your essay, particularly in the exam where time is limited, is to take the title, draw a balloon around it and then brainstorm ideas for your essay.

Example

Consider the following exemplar material, which uses Arthur Miller's *A View From the Bridge* as the drama text.

Task

> Choose a play in which the central character is involved in conflict. Briefly outline the nature of the conflict and then in more detail explain how it helped illustrate the theme(s) of the play. In your answer you should deal with at least two of the following: setting, characterisation, dialogue, key incident, theme, or any appropriate feature.

Top Tip

Brainstorming ideas simply involves focusing on a given topic and then writing down all the connections your mind can make. You may decide to discard some of the ideas or others may occur to you later but the process is a good technique for planning an essay.

Plan

An appropriate title and plan here might be:

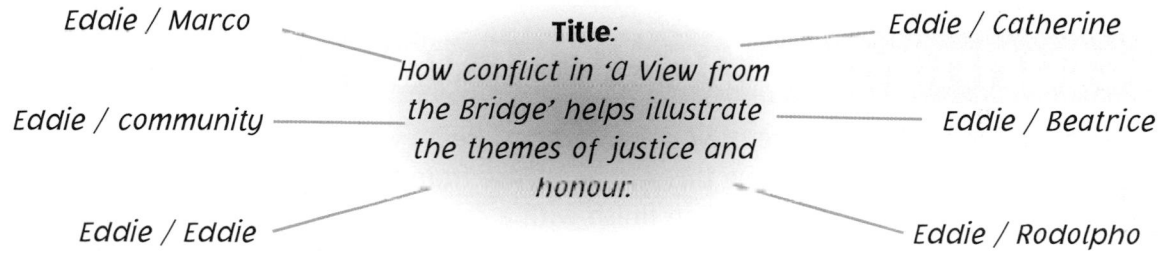

Eddie / Marco

Eddie / community

Eddie / Eddie

Title:
How conflict in 'A View from the Bridge' helps illustrate the themes of justice and honour.

Eddie / Catherine

Eddie / Beatrice

Eddie / Rodolpho

Once you have got some ideas down on paper, you can decide the best order in which to deal with them (perhaps number them on your plan). Combined with your opening paragraph and your conclusion – both of which are essential – you are now ready to tackle the actual essay writing.

Writing your opening paragraph

Remember, the title is not part of your essay, so in your opening paragraph you need to focus in on the task. To do this, take the words of the question and reshape them into an opening statement. Give the title of the text, the author and make reference to the task.

Example

> *A play in which the central character is involved in conflict is 'A View From the Bridge' by Arthur Miller. In this essay I will briefly outline the nature of the conflict and then in more detail explain how it helped illustrate the themes of the play. In my answer I will deal with setting and characterisation.*

Doing this creates a perfectly acceptable opening paragraph.

Using the language of the question in your opening paragraph creates specific purpose to your essay and sets up a clear approach to the task. As you become used to writing critical essays you should try to develop a slightly more sophisticated method of using the task to create your opening paragraph (see the example below) but the essentials remain the same.

Alternative example

'A View From the Bridge' by Arthur Miller is a play concerned with a number of themes, with justice and the law and honour being two of the key issues. The various conflicts within the play help illustrate these themes and our appreciation of these concerns is further enhanced by the setting of the play and by the characterisation of Eddie Carbone, the central figure.

After your opening paragraph you should continue to develop your response, using a clear line of argument/ thought.

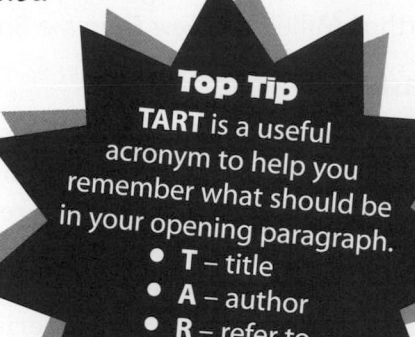

Top Tip
TART is a useful acronym to help you remember what should be in your opening paragraph.
- **T** – title
- **A** – author
- **R** – refer to
- **T** - task

Structuring the body of your essay

Pay particular attention to the structure of your paragraphs. Begin with a statement relevant to the question; follow this with evidence from the text; explain the evidence you have cited; and then finish with a comment linked to the task. This pattern will establish a successful line of thought and also help you meet the other performance criteria.

- **S** Statement
- **E** Evidence
- **E** Explanation
- **C** Comment

Top Tip
SEEC is also a useful mnemonic to help you plan out your paragraphs.

Example

Statement

The character of Eddie Carbone is central to the action of the play. Eddie is seen as an honest hardworking docker of modest ambition.

Evidence

Near the start of the play we are given a summary of Eddie's character by Alfieri, the lawyer and chorus within the play: 'he was as good a man as he had to be in a life that was hard and even'.

Explanation

He speaks of being 'honoured' by the fact that he is in a position to offer shelter to his wife's cousins, Rodolpho and Marco, who arrive as illegal immigrants to the USA. He is indeed honoured, remembering his own father's life.

Comment

Yet by the end of the play Eddie has betrayed not only his household and community but also his former self.

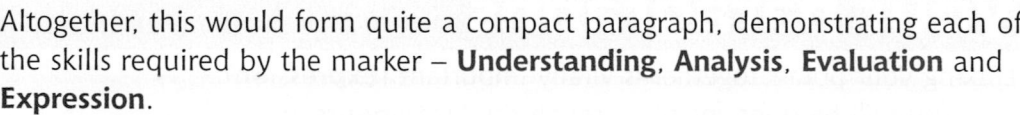
Altogether, this would form quite a compact paragraph, demonstrating each of the skills required by the marker – **Understanding**, **Analysis**, **Evaluation** and **Expression**.

> *The character of Eddie Carbone is central to the action of the play. Eddie is seen as an honest hardworking docker of modest ambition. Near the start of the play we are given a summary of Eddie's character by Alfieri, the lawyer and chorus within the play: 'he was as good a man as he had to be in a life that was hard and even'. He speaks of being 'honoured' by the fact that he is in a position to offer shelter to his wife's cousins, Rodolpho and Marco, who arrive as illegal immigrants to the USA. He is indeed honoured, remembering his own father's life. Yet by the end of the play Eddie has betrayed not only his household and community but also his former self.*

Consider this much more developed paragraph, which still broadly relates to SEEC:

> *A key incident in the play is when Eddie telephones the Immigration Bureau to report the presence of Rodolpho and Marco. Earlier in the play Eddie told the story of Vinny Bolzano as a warning to Catherine. Vinny had revealed the illegal presence of an uncle to the Immigration Bureau. As a result Vinny's family brutally cast him out, refusing to have any further dealings with him. Ironically, Eddie warns Catherine against loose talk: 'Just remember kid, you can quicker get back a million dollars that was stole than a word that you gave away'. In an attempt to thwart the romance between Rodolpho and Catherine, however, he commits a similar act of betrayal, not just against his family but also against the code of honour amongst the Italian community. This tragic degeneration in Eddie's character graphically illustrates the power that his sub-conscious desire for Catherine yields, acting as a motivating force behind all his actions. It is beyond his control, partly because he cannot confront it directly. Ironically the pursuit of this internal passion leads to the complete rejection of Eddie by Catherine who previously held him in the highest regard: 'He's a rat. He belongs in the sewer ... In the garbage he belongs.'*

Top Tip

SEEC is not a four-sentence formula. It will often take two or three sentences to make an effective statement and the evidence and evaluation parts will certainly be more extended. SEEC is a general shape for each paragraph.

Linking your paragraphs

Linking your points together is vitally important (**Expression**). This will be done mainly through the **Statements**, which create your line of thought. In a good critical essay, the **topic sentences** of each paragraph when linked together should provide a **clear** and **logical sequence** of argument. A good test for your own work is to highlight your statements and then read them sequentially as if they were a single paragraph. If there isn't a sense of flow, your line of thought is weak.

Example

The final scene of the play confirms the power of passion as a catalyst to human action. As a result of his telephone call Eddie finds himself in conflict with Marco, the elder of the two cousins who was working to support his wife and family back in Italy. Marco accused Eddie in front of the whole neighbourhood of betraying him: 'That one! He killed my children! That one stole the food from my children'. Eddie's neighbours and friends turn away from him as he has betrayed the unwritten code of his community.

Outwith this tight-knit Italian community that he lives in Eddie has no existence, no point of reference to assure himself of his own identity. He is consumed by a different passion now, a need to force Marco to return his 'name' in order that he, Eddie Carbone, can hold his head up and live with respect in his own neighbourhood. In the final fight scene he demands of Marco, 'I want my name Marco. Now gimme my name ...' In the ensuing struggle Eddie is killed with his own knife.

Commenting on his death Alfieri says 'Now we settle for half' suggesting that the type of blood vendetta that led Marco to seek honour through revenging himself upon Eddie is a thing of the past but he also comments that Eddie's openness as a human being – 'he allowed himself to be wholly known' – appeals to him although it also scares him.

The underlined sections indicate how topics and paragraphs can be easily linked to create a flowing and lucid essay.

Top Tip
Another 'mnemonic' you might find useful, and which is printed on all your exam papers, is **SQA**(!) – **Statement, Quotation, Analysis.**

Exemplar essay

Introduction

Consider the following critical essay, written by a Fifth Year candidate.
How successful has she been in adopting the approach outlined above?
Try identifying the task set, the **Statement-Evidence-Explanation-Comment**
structure of the paragraphs, and also the linkage used.

*'Hotel Room, 12th Floor' by Norman MacCaig is a poem in
which MacCaig outlines his view of modern day society.
The final stanza of the poem makes a significant
statement as it reflects the central idea of the poem,
explored through imagery and word choice, that evil is
within us and we are no more civilised now than at the
time of the Wild West.*

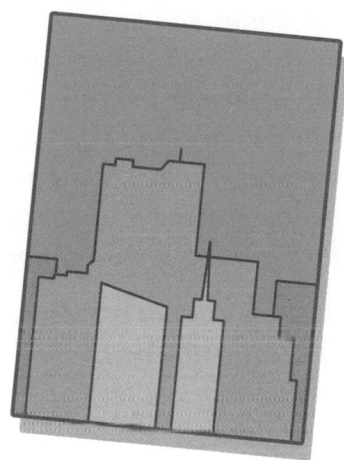

*The concluding lines of the poem are a comment on
everything that MacCaig has seen and heard and they
reveal his thoughts on the American way of life:*

> *'The frontier is never
> somewhere else. And no stockades
> can keep midnight out.'*

*These two sentences reflect the imagery, mood and ideas
that are present throughout the poem and they
effectively conclude the poem, expressing the central
idea that MacCaig is trying to put across that civilisation
depends on the individual decisions that we all make
about how we wish to behave.*

*In this final stanza MacCaig attacks the 'stockades', the buildings, cities
and technology that have been built to represent civilisation, as being
insufficient to modify human behaviour. His use of imagery throughout
the poem has already suggested this idea. In stanza one he describes a
helicopter as 'skirting like a damaged insect the Empire State Building'
which he describes as a 'jumbo size dentist's drill'. Both a helicopter
and the Empire State Building are normally viewed with wonder and
awe but yet MacCaig has related them to suffering. The simile and
metaphor used are extremely effective in revealing his thoughts. 'A
helicopter skirting like a damaged insect' is successful because it shows
how small and insignificant the helicopter seems compared to the
massive buildings surrounding it. Norman MacCaig is also implying that
the sound made by a helicopter is not pleasant, similar to that of a
damaged insect buzzing. The image also illustrates how the helicopter is
continually going round in circles and not getting anywhere. A damaged
insect creates irritating noises and pointlessly repeats the tracks that it
has just covered. MacCaig creates an unpleasant image in the reader's
mind.*

His use of the metaphor shares similar purpose to the simile. The Empire State Building is described as 'that jumbo size dentist's drill' which exhibits MacCaig's feeling to what was the biggest building in the world at the time he wrote the poem. A dentist drill is an effective instrument used to compare the building to especially since the top of both the drill and the building are the same shape. However, the underlying meaning of the use of the drill is to show MacCaig's contempt towards the idea of big buildings and is a criticism of the American desire to have the biggest of everything. A dentist's drill is a common metaphor for pain and suffering and MacCaig has used it well to show his dislike for the Empire State Building or more generally over-sized buildings. The two conceits used are subtly referred back to in the last stanza: 'no stockades can keep midnight out'. Midnight is the symbolism for the lack of civilisation or for evil and the stockades are what MacCaig believes as the pretence that civilisation exists. Helicopters, the Empire State Building and the Pan Am skyscraper which is also mentioned are all the stockades that have been built as a cover for the evil that exists within people. I believe that MacCaig has shown his disdain for the stockades through the mocking imagery of two unpleasant illustrations.

However, although MacCaig portrays daytime New York as unpleasant his illustration of night-time is a more sinister and evil picture. In the despairing last line of the poem MacCaig concludes the idea examined of good and religion fighting evil and has shows the main idea of the poem that evil is existing still in people despite efforts to create civilisation. At the end of the first stanza MacCaig states that

> 'The uncivilised darkness
> is shot as by a million lit windows, all
> ups and acrosses.'

The lit windows shooting at the darkness may be thought of as religion combating evil. The windows are all 'ups and acrosses', the shape of the cross and represents Christ dying to save civilisation. This religious aspect is an idea that MacCaig is presenting as a vain attempt to defeat evil. In the last line he states that 'no stockades can keep midnight out'. He is saying that religion and goodness have failed and that evil prevails. It is a pessimistic view but is the central idea of 'Hotel Room, 12th Floor' and I believe that MacCaig has clearly presented his point through the idea of the light (religion and goodness) fighting darkness (evil and sin).

In the penultimate sentence of the poem the frontier mentioned is an extension of the Wild West theme that MacCaig uses to express how civilisation in not moving on. He describes that he lies in bed in between the television and radio and hears:

> 'the wildest of warhoops continually ululating through
> the glittering canyons and gulches'

The alliteration used intensifies the noises that he is hearing, the noises of what would've been the Indians in the western films. The 'glittering canyons and gulches' refers to the streets and the bright neon lights of New York City. A dash is then used which links the Wild West to New York by talking about what is happening in the streets of where MacCaig is:

> 'police cars and ambulances racing
> to the broken bones, the harsh screaming
> from coldwater flats, the blood
> glazed on sidewalks.'

The choice of words, 'broken bones' is a use of synecdoche that has been used to make the injury seem common and to depersonalise it. The screaming from the poverty of the New York flats and the blood that has glazed over because nobody has cared to clean it up are showing the madness of the life in today's world. MacCaig is showing that the old western films that are on the television are no different from today. 'The frontier is never somewhere else', the evil is within us and MacCaig believes that this doesn't disappear with bright lights and big buildings. The Wild West theme is used to examine the differences in civilisation between then and now and MacCaig has come to the conclusion that people are still the same and has shown this by reflecting on all his Wild West comparisons in the final stanza.

The concluding verse of the poem gives no solution to the lack of civilisation and therefore MacCaig is saying that religion and goodness have failed. Unlike western films where good always prevails MacCaig is saying that real life is maybe not so black and white. Throughout, the poem attacks New York but in the final stanza he comments that 'the frontier is never somewhere else' and makes the idea of evil more universal. He believes that 'no stockades can keep midnight out' and there is no hope for man if it is naively thought that development of civility is by new technology or bigger buildings.

MacCaig has clearly outlined his views of modern day society in 'Hotel Room, 12th Floor'. His view on the global pretence of civilisation is clearly expressed in his word choice and imagery and the final stanza of the poem acts as a significant moment that reveals the true meaning of the poem that evil lies within people and the way we choose to behave is what causes a hole in our civilisation.

Essay topics

Introduction

Listed below are Intermediate 2 style assignments for critical essay writing. Try planning out answers for the texts you are studying and even writing some of the essays.

Before each section of the paper there will be boxed advice to the candidate, reminding you that answers to questions should refer to the text and to appropriate relevant features. The **Drama** section, for example, may highlight areas such as characterisation, key scene, structure, climax, conflict, setting... The **Prose** section may talk about characterisation, setting, key incidents, plot structure, theme... **Poetry** will highlight areas such as word choice, tone, imagery, rhythm...

Top Tip
The boxed advice about features of the text is a useful reminder to you of some of the areas you should be covering in your answer but remeber to stay focused on the question itself.

Drama

Choose a play where conflict is central to the plot.

Briefly explain the nature of the conflict and then in more detail show how it is resolved, or not, by the end of the play.

Prose

Choose a novel or short story where the main character changes in the course of the story.

By examining this change in detail, show how it affects your understanding of the character.

Poetry

Choose a poem which takes either a pessimistic or an optimistic view of life.

Briefly state what the poem is about and then show how the writer's use of poetic techniques helped you understand the poem's meaning.

Active learning – group discussion

Discussion is not part of the formal assessment of your course but it is recognised by the SQA in its guidance notes that group discussion is an **essential feature** of any English course as it is one of the most frequently used methods of **exploring texts and topics** in the classroom.

Taking part in the discussion is about more than sitting listening. However interesting you find the comments made by your classmates, if you do not contribute to the discussion you will gain very little from it.

Don't be afraid to **ask questions** – other people may have an answer that helps your understanding.

And don't be afraid to **express your own views** – try out ideas that are in your head to see what other students think of them but remember, when you are making a contribution try to back up your opinions with evidence.

Body language is part of the dynamics in a group discussion: look at the person who is talking and let them know that you are listening and when you are speaking try to make eye contact with the other members of the group.

Learning is an **active process** and group discussion an excellent approach to stimulating thought and analysis. That's why teachers use it so much in class. But you need to **participate** to gain from it – so don't sit back, **speak up!**

Top Tip
Discussing ideas with other members of your class is an excellent way of developing opinions on a given topic or text but quite often, ideas will be forgotten if they are not written down, so it is useful to make a few notes for your own use of any key points arising out of group talk.

Written response

Introduction

In this compulsory unit you will need to read and study a text of your own choice and then respond critically to the ideas contained within it. Text can be interpreted fairly generously and in theory you could study fairly specialist areas or treat text as a reference to film or other media products.

Most students, however, choose a novel as their source material (or occasionally a drama script or poetry) and the following advice is based on that choice, although it can be applied equally to the more specialist options.

Purpose of the assessment

The key purpose of the personal study assessment is to test your ability to **respond thoughtfully** and **independently to a piece of literature**. It tests your **communication skills** by assessing your **writing (or talk)**.

What you have to do

You will be required to write (or talk) about your text using a framework – **task** – previously agreed by yourself and your teacher. The written assessment will be completed **within a single hour** and will be tackled under **controlled conditions**.

You are allowed notes to assist you with the writing: **two sides of A4 paper** in total. You are also allowed to have the text with you.

The same four key criteria apply as for the critical essay:

Understanding

Demonstrate your understanding of the **key aspects** and main issues of the text(s) studied by **identifying significant sections** in the text(s).

Analysis

Explain how aspects of the writing, such as **characterisation** and **structure**, contribute to the meaning and impact of the text. This will require relevant quotations or references to details in the text to support any comments you make.

Evaluation

Comment on what **you thought** about the text and judge how **effective** you feel the **writer was in conveying** or **exploring** a particular issue. The main requirement in making an evaluation is to justify what you are saying by reference to the text.

Expression

This is about **assessing your writing skills**. How well have you **expressed** your point of view? Is your essay **well-organised**? Have you presented a **clear line of thought** in your argument?

Some suggestions for personal study reading are contained in **Appendix B** (see pages 92–95).

How to tackle the personal study

The key to a good personal study essay is to have a **planned** and **prepared** **approach** to the text. Your teacher can discuss various ways of approaching your essay and offer advice on your suggestions but he/she is not allowed to create your task for you, as the assessment is about your ability to think critically about your chosen text.

Use the **SEEC** approach discussed on page 70 – it will help you to structure your essay and organise your notes.

There are, however, some preliminary steps to follow before we are ready to discuss the writing stage.

- Your choice of book is vitally important. **Novels** are most frequently chosen by candidates but you are free to choose other options such as **poetry**, **drama** and **non-fiction**. The novel, however, should be familiar territory for most candidates through your Standard Grade folio and book reports from lower down the school.

- In theory, you are free to choose any text but it is important that you pick one of some **literary merit** as this will provide you with more substance for your essay. 'Light' reads, such as books from a formulaic series, tend to have weaker characterisation and simplified plots and as a result there is less for you to analyse and comment on.

- Once you have chosen your text, **read through it** as soon as you can and form an initial response to the text.

- After you have finished the book give some thought to what **aspect of the text** you intend to **focus** on. You will not be writing a general book review. This will require you to think about issues such as **theme**, **characterisation**, **structure** and **setting**.

- The more focused your task, the better your essay will be.

- Having decided on the focus of your essay, you should **re-read** the text. Consider carefully the **themes** being explored by the writer and **make full notes** to help you write your essay: for example, list important incidents in the story, make pen sketches of the key characters, outline key details relating to setting, and so on.

- Be sure to **identify key quotations** to use in your essay.

- When this is done, you are ready to **plan the writing stage**.

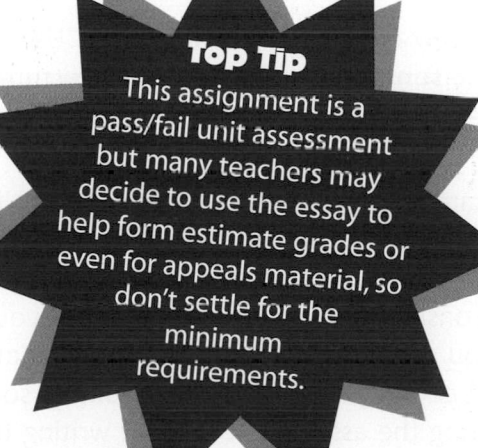

Top Tip
This assignment is a pass/fail unit assessment but many teachers may decide to use the essay to help form estimate grades or even for appeals material, so don't settle for the minimum requirements.

Writing an essay

Creating a task

As with any critical essay, the first stage is to create a title that reflects the purpose of your essay. For example:

> *How Anne Donovan's use of Scots in her novel 'Buddha Da', aided my enjoyment and understanding of the novel.*

or

> *How the unusual narrative stance of Anne Donovan's 'Buddha Da', aided my understanding of the novel's characterisation.*

or

> *How Mark Haddon's 'The Curious Incident Of The Dog In The Night-time' effectively examines human relationships.*

or

> *How the detailed description in Joe Simpson's 'Touching the Void', successfully conveyed the emotions and tension of the experience being described.*

Note from the first two examples that the alternative tasks for the same book will create **two quite different essays**. You must be clear about the **purpose** of your essay.

Having decided on a title, **brainstorm** some ideas around it.

multiple narrators   *How the unusual narrative stance of Anne Donovan's 'Buddha Da', aided my enjoyment and understanding of the novel.*   *insight to character of Anne Marie*

insight to character of Jimmy   *insight to character of Liz*

impact on narrative/plot

You can now create your **outline plan**. Use **statements** and **topic sentences** to create your structure. These sentences should link together to shape your line of thought.

In an exam situation the time factor might limit you to ballooning the title and brainstorming some ideas but as you are allowed two pages of notes you should consider a more detailed plan for your personal study. You should certainly have your **quotations selected** and **key statements** formulated so that your time during the assessment is spent writing the essay rather than planning it or searching for references from the text.

Top Tip
Remember that your personal study text may be used in the exam to respond to a critical essay question but if you choose to do this be certain that you are responding to the task set in the exam paper and not rewriting your personal study essay.

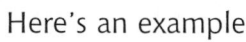

Here's an example.

NOTES

Introduction

Title & Author – A. Donovan – 'Buddha Da'

Reference to Task – Multiple narrative stance/insight into each character's feelings

Para 1

Statement – The novel begins with Anne Marie as the first-person narrator.

Evidence – 'Ma Da' a nutter. Radio rental. He'd dae anything for a laugh so he wid ...'

'He's turnt into a Buddhist.'

Explanation – Scots – real voice; reference to 'Da' and idea of possibility of doing something stupid; various examples and then punchline.

Comment - Creates persona for Anne Marie, starts key plot line for novel

Para 2

Using Anne Marie as the narrator allows the writer to colour the scenes being described with Anne Marie's own reactions and understanding.

Evidence – 'I've never seen ma da lookin' like that afore; there wis a kinda faraway look in his eyes'.

Explanation – AM struck by the seriousness of her Da.

Comment – clear to see how AM trying to understand the changes being talked about.

Essay

The above would lead to something like this for the opening paragraphs:

Anne Donovan's novel 'Buddha Da' employs a multiple narrative stance with each of the three central characters, members of the same family, telling parts of the tale from their own perspective. As a result we are able to understand in a very direct way, each of the character's feelings and reactions to the key decision of one of them - Jimmy, the 'Da' - to become a Buddhist and the subsequent impact on their lives. The structure of the novel made it both highly readable and authentic.

The novel begins with Anne Marie, the daughter, as the first-person narrator. Our attention is immediately caught with the opening lines; 'Ma Da's a nutter. Radio rental. He'd dae anything for a laugh so he wid ...' Donovan's use of Scots gives Anne Marie's character an immediate authenticity. The use of colloquialism such as 'Radio rental' adds to the impact of the character and creates a certain warmth about her. When Anne Marie goes on to tell us that her Da's latest escapade beats everything that he's done before, 'He's turnt intae a Buddhist', the stage is set for the impact of this decision to roll out across the lives of the characters.

Using Anne Marie as the narrator allows the writer to colour the scenes being described with Anne Marie's own reactions and understanding. As she listens to her Dad trying to explain to his wife that he is serious Anne Marie comments, 'I've never seen ma da lookin' like that afore; there wis a kinda faraway look in his eyes.' It's clear that Anne Marie is struck by the seriousness of her Dad although she is still not convinced that he'll follow through his idea. The method of narration, however, personalises the impact of the Dad's decision and even in this small example it clear to see how Anne Marie is trying to understand the changes being talked about.

Spoken response

Introduction

You have the option to deliver your personal study assessment as a spoken response. Uptake of this option in schools is relatively small as it requires a considerable amount of class time to carry out the assessments. Some advice is given below, however, for those pursuing this alternative.

Top Tip

If your school awards cerificates for Core Skills, a spoken response for Personal Study covers the Talk requirement.

Purpose of the assessment

The purpose of the assessment is the same as for a written response: to test your ability to **respond thoughtfully** and **independently to a piece of literature**, only in this case it is your talking communication skills that are being assessed.

What you have to do

The assessment takes the form of a delivered talk, which must last **at least four minutes** and be followed by in-depth questions from an audience of **no less than three people**. All performance criteria related to the task must be met during the course of the talk. **Understanding**, **Analysis** and **Evaluation** are essentially the same as for a written response (see page 78). **Expression** and **Interaction with Audience** are detailed below.

Expression

This is about the **performance** side of your presentation. Speech should be **clear** and **audible** and you should make effective use of **both verbal** and **non-verbal techniques** to deliver the talk, for example, varying the **intonation of your voice** and using **gestures** and **body language**.

Interaction with audience

This is essentially about **responding to questions** asked and being **aware of audience** reaction during your talk to audience responses (for example, pausing for laughter rather than carrying on).

How to tackle spoken personal study

As with any assessment, success depends on adequate preparation. The steps outlined above for a written personal study – **reading**, **re-reading and preparing notes** – apply equally for spoken presentation.

Planning the talk is also similar to planning an essay.

Devise a **planning title** and then **create a mind map** of your ideas and thoughts around this focus.

Like an essay, a talk will benefit enormously from having a **clear structure**.

List the various headings you intend to cover during the talk, as with your **statements (topic sentences)**. Concentrate on the **key issues** and look to develop them thoroughly rather than having a long list of topics that are skimmed over.

Make sure that each element of the talk is introduced with a **key statement**, and that you **link the sections** together with appropriate phrases.

In a **written** personal study your **writing ability** is also being assessed; and in a **spoken** personal study, your **talk skills** are being tested. So **do not, under any circumstances, bury your nose in your notes and read from a word-by-word script**. You will have notes to assist you but they should be abbreviated and act as an **aid to memory** rather than be the full content of the speech.

Before delivering your talk – **practise**. Use your parents, your brother/sister, the family dog, the mirror – whatever, as long as you rehearse the talk before delivering it. And practise does not mean only once!

Finally, a few reminders.

Top Tip
It can be very useful to tape yourself delivering a talk and then to listen to how the talk sounds. Are you saying what you think you are saying?

- Speak clearly and maintain an even pace. It is not a race!
- Look at your audience and engage with them.
- Show you are interested in what you are saying, as your enthusiasm will support the presentation.
- And remember, with careful preparation, the talk will take care of itself.

Active learning – revision

Organising notes

- For each text you study, you will build up a set of **notes**, based on **classwork**, **group discussions**, **teacher comment** and **your own work**.

- To make full use of your notes for study and revision, it is important that they do not remain '**static**' but instead provide the basis for active thinking about the text.

- When students simply read and re-read notes over and over they begin to 'learn' them parrot-fashion and this actually **weakens** their own ability to think creatively and lucidly about the text. This results in tired critical essays which may demonstrate sufficient knowledge about a text but which are usually lacking in relevant understanding and analysis. As a result, they are weaker in responding to the actual task, as notes are simply being regurgitated without thought.

- To avoid this trap, actively **reorganise and expand your basic notes** as you revise.

As indicated above, you will not be starting revision from scratch, as notes will have been gathered from various sources.

Top Tip

There are a number of educational websites that offer good revision notes on various texts. You should make use of these sites as part of your revision but remember that plagiarism is heavily penalised by the SQA.

Questions to ask yourself

The following generic questions can be used as a worksheet to help you tackle most texts:

Drama and prose

Setting – where and when is the story set? In what way is this significant?

Storyline – what are the main stages in the development of the actual plot? In particular, which incident is the key turning point for the central characters?

Characterisation – a basic character sketch for prose and drama will answer the following questions:

- **Who** is the character? (name, background, relationships, characteristics)
- **What** does he/she do? (consider also the consequences of his/her actions)
- **Why** does he/she do this?
- What is the main **change** for the central character(s)? In what way is he/she different as a result of what has happened?

Theme – what issue is the writer trying to make us think about? How does the writer use setting and storyline to present this issue to us? What other techniques does the writer use to convey his/her theme (language, incident, imagery, symbolism, structure ...)?

Poetry

Some of the above questions can also be applied to poetry, particularly the issue of **setting in time and place**.

Time of writing/genre – it is useful to know when a poem was written, as assignments will sometimes make reference to, for example, pre-twentieth century poetry. It is also useful to know if the poem belongs to a particular genre of poetry: narrative, sonnet, free verse, and so on.

Key theme – what is the key theme of the poem?

Stance – what stance has the poet taken - personal, detached observer, dramatised persona, and so on.

Structure – how does the structure of the poem aid our understanding?

Literary techniques – which literary techniques does the poet use to explore his/her theme? This will certainly include the poet's choice of words and use of figurative language and imagery. (See Appendix A, page 88.)

Top Tip

Many students learn poems 'off by heart'. While this ensures an ample source of quotations, remember that it is analysis and comment in response to the task that create a good essay, not the memorising of an entire poem.

Listing quotations

For each of the texts you have studied you should have a prepared list of **quotations** that you have memorised for use in your essay.

For each quotation you should be **clear** where it came from and **what point(s)** you might be able to make from it.

The following list might form a suitable set of quotations, for example, if you have studied John Steinbeck's *Of Mice and Men*.

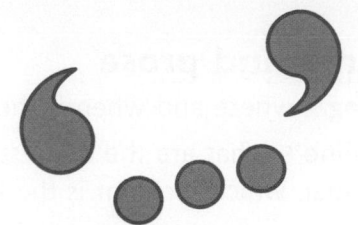

'(He) was small and quick, dark of face, with restless eyes and sharp, strong features. Every part of him was defined: small strong hands, slender arms, a thin and bony nose.'
– description of George.

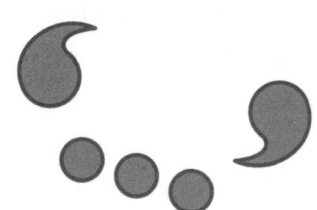

'A huge man, shapeless of face, with large, pale eyes, with wide, sloping shoulders; and he walked heavily, dragging his feet a little, the way a bear drags his paws.'
– description of Lennie.

George says, 'Guys like us, that work on ranches, are the loneliest guys in the world.'
– start of the 'dream' story, supports the theme of loneliness.

Lennie says, 'But not us – An' why? Because ... because I've got you to look after me, and you got me to look after you, and that's why.'
– discussing the 'dream', supports the friendship between the two men.

'We got somebody to talk to that gives a damn about us.'
– the dream again, supports George and Lennie's friendship

Curley's wife talking to Crooks, 'I could get you strung up on a tree so easy it ain't even funny.'
– illustration of both the racism in the novel and Curley's wife's character.

'I got hurt four year ago ... They'll can me purty soon.'
– Candy, explaining why he wants to join George and Lennie; lack of purpose in the lives of ranch-hands.

'You're nuts ... But you're a kinda nice fella. Jus' like a big baby'
– Curley's wife, talking to Lennie – build up to Lennie killing Curley's wife, summarises Lennie's innocence.

'God a'mighty, if I was alone I could live so easy.'
– George complaining about looking after Lennie; insight into George's character.

'Coulda been in the movies, an' had nice clothes – all them nice clothes like they wear.'
– Curley's wife's dream, reveals her loneliness, also.

'A guy needs somebody – to be near him ... I tell ya a guy gets too lonely, an' he gets sick.'
– Crooks talking to Lennie, theme of racism and loneliness.

'Some day – we're gonna get the jack together and we're gonna have a little house and a couple of acres an' a cow and some pigs ... an live off the fatta the lan'.'
– George and Lennie's dream – key theme of the novel.

'I ain't gonna let them hurt Lennie.'
– when George finds out about Lennie killing Curley's wife; foreshadows George's actions in killing Lennie at the end.

Top Tip
Not every quotation will suit every question so make sure that you have a variety of quotations learned and certainly more than you would expect to use in a single essay.

Critical terminology

List of terms

Alliteration – the use of the same consonant sound, usually at the beginning of words, for example, 'soft snow settled on the silent scene', 'funny phone'.

Ambiguity – the idea that a word or phrase might mean more than one thing. Used in poetry to develop multiple levels of interpretation.

Clause – the grammatical term for a unit of language consisting of a verb and the words associated with it.

Cliché – an overused expression, often figurative, which has lost its impact because of its frequent use, for example, 'A game of two halves'.

Conjunction – a word that links or joins together two words, phrases or clauses, for example, 'and'.

Connotation – the ideas that might be suggested by a particular word choice, for example, 'He meandered into the room'. 'Meandered' here suggests a lack of purpose.

Content – the ideas contained within a text.

Context – the words, phrases, sentences around the specified expression/word.

Course – a course comprises the individual units of a given subject, with their assessments, combined with the external examination.

Enjambment – where a poet runs a sentence or expression over more than one line without pause, e.g. consider these lines from Margaret Taylor's *Loneliness* (see page 54) where this technique is used:

> I must have walked this road
> This endless road
> A thousand years,

Figurative Language – language that makes use of figures of speech and various techniques to add extra meaning to a text through a non-literal interpretation. Common figures of speech include metaphors, similes and personification.

Genre – a type or category of text, for example, prose, drama, poetry, media.

Hyperbole – the proper term for deliberate exaggeration in writing, usually to provoke a reaction from the reader. 'If I have told you that once, I have told you a million times.'

Image – the picture that is created by the words, often carrying some further meaning, for example, the image of a rose has connotations of beauty.

Irony – this is a frequently used technique and it involves the idea of opposites but unlike sarcasm, explained later, it is not always negative in nature. Dramatic irony might involve a character saying something on stage that the audience knows will not come true. Irony can come from a situation where the intention of a charactcr ends up with the opposite happening. It can be humorous, tragic, sad, fortunate or bitter:

'The irony of the situation was that the guide to understanding English only served to confuse the student more!'

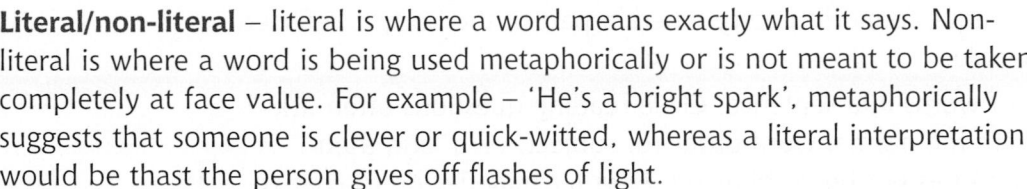

Literal/non-literal – literal is where a word means exactly what it says. Non-literal is where a word is being used metaphorically or is not meant to be taken completely at face value. For example – 'He's a bright spark', metaphorically suggests that someone is clever or quick-witted, whereas a literal interpretation would be thast the person gives off flashes of light.

Litotes – deliberate understatement used to create a particular effect. For example, 'The school football squad is not the strongest group of players in the world', meaning it is one of the weakest!

Metaphor – a comparison where the object being described is referred to directly as if it was something else, rather than being 'like' it. For example, 'The diamond-studded sky twinkled overhead' is comparing the stars to diamonds, but does not make a direct link in the way that a simile would: 'The stars, which were like diamonds in the sky, twinkled overhead.'

Onomatopoela – where a word makes the sound it is describing, for example, 'sizzle', 'thud'.

Oxymoron – used to describe two words which are contradictory but which used together express a clear meaning, for example, 'bitter sweet'. ('Easy exam' might be a phrase that most students would regard as an oxymoron!)

Paradox – a puzzling contradiction of opposites; two contradictory ideas linked together. An example is the saying, 'You always hurt the one you love'.

Paragraph – a group of sentences about the same topic.

Parenthesis – a word or phrase that is not an essential part of the sentence, but is included to provide additional information or make an aside. Can be created by the use of two dashes, brackets or a pair of commas.

Personification – where an inanimate object is described as having qualities normally associated with something that is alive: 'The wind whistled down the alley' or 'Winter spread its icy grip over the fields and hills'.

Portmanteau – a term first used by Lewis Carroll to describe a word which has been created by joining together two existing words, for example, eugenics and genesis to create eugenesis; or lithe and slimy to give slithy.

Sarcasm – to do with the tone of a text or expression. It is usually identified when the opposite of what is being said is what is actually meant. Sarcasm is often a criticism of some sort, for example saying 'That was very clever!' when you actually mean 'That was incredibly stupid!'

Sentence – a group of words that make sense; almost always centred on a verb.

Simile – where two or more things are compared directly using the word 'like' or 'as' to link the comparison, for example, 'The stars were like diamonds in the sky.'

Stanza – refers to poetry where groups of lines are used to structure the poem.

Syllable – a group of letters that combine to make a sound (think of the party game Charades). For example, beautiful has three syllables – **beau – ti – ful** – but ugly has only two – **ug – ly**.

Symbol – an idea or object that represents more than just its literal self, for example, light is often a symbol of hope.

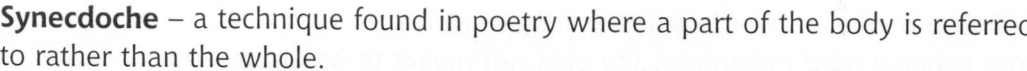
Synecdoche – a technique found in poetry where a part of the body is referred to rather than the whole.

Syntax – the order of words in a sentence. Close reading questions often ask about sentences where the normal word order (of subject, verb, and then additional information) has not been followed. A writer may decide to change this structure in order to create a particular effect or emphasis: for example, by beginning with an adverb, 'Nervously, the candidate entered the exam room'.

Theme – the central concern of a text; the idea being explored rather than the events of the text.

Tone – the feel, sense of atmosphere suggested by words; in speech the sound of someone's voice conveys tone quite clearly but its meaning is essentially the same whether the words are spoken or written. Look back at the close reading passages for examples of tone (see pages 18–35).

Unit – National Qualification courses in English are divided into three separate units: **Language**, **Literature** and **Personal Study**. A student can be accredited with passes in a single unit but to achieve a course pass all three units must be passed as well as the external examination.

Verse – refers to separate sections of a poem, often with a distinct rhyming scheme.

Parts of Speech

Adjective – adjectives describe nouns and are often found before the noun (or before another adjective if more than one is being used), for example, 'the red, crumbling brick wall'.
(**Note** – in a different context, red could be a noun – how a word is used defines its function.)

Adverb – a word which modifies a verb in some way, for example, 'He ran quickly'. 'Quickly' tells us more about the verb.

Noun – a word which names things. There are different types of noun:

- **proper nouns** give the names of actual **places** or **persons**, for example, Glasgow, Marianna, Britney Spears

- **common nouns** refer to **objects**, for example, desks, floor, rivers

- **collective nouns** define **groups of things**, for example, herd, class

- **abstract nouns** define **qualities**, for example, wisdom, kindness.

Pronoun – a pronoun is a word which replaces a noun, for example, he, she, it, they.

Verb – a verb is often referred to as a 'doing word' and if you know what this means you know what a verb is; the word which denotes the action, for example, run, cry, shout.

Punctuation

Apostrophe (') – used to indicate where a letter has been missed out when two words are contracted together, for example, it's = it is; or to show when something belongs to another (shows possession) for example, Sheila's house = the house that belongs to Sheila.

Colon (:) – used to introduce a list or occasionally to balance two clauses, of equal importance, which might otherwise require to be two separate sentences.

Comma (,) – used to create a pause in a sentence and to break up a list of items. Also used in parenthesis.

Exclamation mark (!) – used to indicate when a word, phrase, clause or sentence should be read as indicating surprise or special emphasis.

Full stop (.) – used to mark the end of a sentence.

Inverted commas (" ") – used to indicate direct speech and to indicate titles. Also used to show where a word is not to be taken literally as its usage is slightly unusual in the given context. Single (' ') or double (" ") inverted commas are usually equally acceptable.

Question mark (?) – used to mark the end of a sentence that asks a question.

Semi-colon (;) – used where a longer pause than a comma is required; usually to indicate an expansion of an idea in the second part of the sentence. Can also be used to break up a list, especially where it is a list of phrases/clauses rather than single words.

Register – the term used to describe groups of words or phrases that are associated with a particular genre, for example, 'Dearly Beloved ... brethren ... amen' would be an example of a **religious** register.

Rhyme – words that have the same sound, used most often at the end of lines in poetry:

> As virtuous men pass mildly away,
> And whisper to their souls, to go,
> Whilst some of their sad friends do say,
> The breath goes now, and some say, no...

> A Valediction Forbidding Mourning
> John Donne

Rhythm – the beat within a line of poetry, created through stressed syllables. Consider this limerick:

> There was a young man from the West
> Who thought he was simply the best
> But there came from the East
> A strange kind of beast
> And history tells us the rest!

The syllables in bold are stressed, giving us the traditional rhythm of a limerick:

> Da **da** da da **da** da da **da**
> Da **da** da da **da** da da **da**
> Da da **da**, da da **da**
> Da **da**, da da **da**
> Da **da** da da **da** da da **da**.

Personal Study reading list

Introduction

Novels tend to be the most popular choice among students for independent study, although you can also choose between non-fiction, poetry and drama. The list below contains a number of suggestions that are popular with teenage readers. If you wish to find out more about particular titles you can either visit a bookshop or use the internet. Most bookshop websites include readers' reviews and a brief synopsis of the book in question.

It is important to select a text that you will enjoy reading because personal engagement is one of the key issues in assessing the quality of critical essay responses, so take your time and choose wisely.

Clearly this list is not exhaustive and it is really only offered by way of a sample of the kind of books you should be looking at. Your teacher will be able to offer you sound advice in your final choice.

Things Fall Apart Chinua Achebe, (Penguin Books, ISBN: 0141186887)
This novel has become a modern classic. It tells the powerful story of Okonkwo, a proud member of the Ibo tribe, and how the culture of his people becomes threatened by the emergence of white colonialism in his country. Lots of material to write about.

The Hitchhiker's Guide to the Galaxy Douglas Adams, (Heinemann, ISBN: 0434003484)
A cultural classic! Join Arthur Dent on a hair-raising tour of the Galaxy. Humorous and off-beat in tone.

Brick Lane Monica Ali, (Black Swan, ISBN: 0552771155)
A Booker prize winning novel that tells the tale of Nazneen – a teenage girl who moves from her Bangladeshi village to London's East End following an arranged marriage.

The War Orphan Rachel Anderson, (Oxford University Press, ISBN: 019275095x)
Simon's family adopt a Vietnamese war orphan, Ha, who has suffered terribly. But Simon has to discover much about himself as he struggles to cope with his new brother's nightmares.

The Crow Road Iain Banks, (Abacus, ISBN: 0349109079)
Prentice McHoan returns home to investigate the mysterious death of an uncle but various temptations distract his attention.

Eon Greg Bear, (Gollancz, ISBN: 0575073160)
A complex science-fiction epic that examines one possibility for our future. One for fans of the genre.

Exodus Julie Bertagna, (Macmillan, ISBN: 033039908X)
Set in 2099, this is the story of Mara and her fellow refugees as they set out to find a new world after melting ice-caps force them to evacuate their island-home.

Noughts and Crosses Malorie Blackman, (Corgi, ISBN: 0552546321)
First in a trilogy, although complete in its own right. In a parallel society the race hatred of our world is mirrored by the divisions and violence between the Noughts and the Crosses. Seph and Callum find their relationship compromised by their circumstances.

Quite Ugly One Morning Christopher Brookmyre, (Abacus, ISBN: 0349108854)
A thriller written with the usual panache from this Scottish writer who lays bare the darker side of human behaviour but always manages to raise a smile from the reader while doing so.

Junk Melvin Burgess, (Puffin Books, ISBN: 0140380191)
The gritty story of Tar and Gemma, two teenage runaways who become involved in serious drug-taking. Popular with teenagers because of the way it tackles real issues in an uncompromising way.

Breakfast at Tiffany's Truman Capote, (Penguin Books, ISBN: 0141182792)
This tale of Holly Golightly, a seemingly carefree and stunningly beautiful young woman, offers wide scope for character analysis in a critical response. A fairly short book.

Do Androids Dream of Electric Sheep? Philip K. Dick, (Orion, ISBN: 0752864300)
A science-fiction classic that spawned the film Bladerunner. Rick Deckard, a bounty hunter, searches for a group of renegade replicants.

The Commitments Roddy Doyle, (Vintage, ISBN: 0749391685)
Part of the Barrytown trilogy that looks at the lives of the Rabbite family from North Dublin. This first tale is that of Jimmy and his attempt to form a rock band. It examines issues such as the individual versus the group and like the other books, *The Snapper* and *The Van*, it is quite an easy book to read while still offering the student a number of sound points to write about.

The Woman Who Walked into Doors Roddy Doyle, (Vintage, ISBN: 0749395990)
A more sombre book from Roddy Doyle which charts the chaotic life of a woman driven to alcoholism by the abuse she suffers from her husband.

The Skin I'm In Sharon Flake, (Corgi, ISBN: 0552547638)
A story about an adolescent coming to terms with her own identity. Strong teenage appeal.

A Million Little Pieces James Frey, (John Murray, ISBN: 0719561027)
A shocking and brutal memoir of how drug addiction can destroy a life.

Sophie's World Jostein Gaarder, (Phoenix, ISBN: 1857992911)
'Who are you? Where does the world come from?' If you want to know the answer to these deep philosophical questions this book is for you – but be warned, it is not an easy journey.

The Beach Alex Garland, (Penguin, ISBN 0140258418)
A first-class adventure story that also raises questions about the values of our society.

The Curious Incident of the Dog In The Night-Time Mark Haddon, (Vintage, ISBN 0099456761)
An amazing book that views the world through the eyes of Christopher, an intelligent boy who is also autistic. Funny and thought-provoking.

Hurricane, The Life of Rubin Carter - Fighter James S. Hirsch, (Fourth Estate, ISBN: 1841151300)
A biographical account of black boxer Rubin Carter, wrongfully imprisoned for murder, and his long struggle for justice.

The Changeling Robin Jenkins, (Canongate Classics, ISBN: 0862412285)
Tom Curdie is what people would describe as a ned. But one of his teachers thinks that there may be more to him, or is the teacher just on an ego trip? Tom goes on holiday with the teacher's family, leaving behind his Glasgow home, but what lies in front? A relatively straightforward book to tackle.

Other Colours Catherine Johnson, (Livewire, ISBN: 0704349450)
This is from the *Livewire for Teenage Readers* series and, like most of the books in the collection, it appeals greatly to young adults. In this novel Louise runs away from her mother and stepfather to find her own identity and ambitions on the streets of London.

Bitter Fruit Brian Keaney, (Orchard Books, ISBN: 1841210056)
Rebecca's father dies in a car accident and the teenager is forced to come to terms with many of life's realities more quickly than she would have otherwise.

A Different Life Lois Keith, (Livewire, ISBN: 0704349469)
Another from the *Livewire* series that tells the story of Libby Starling who becomes disabled at the age of fifteen. Suddenly she has to reassess her life and her attitude. More crucially she has to deal with the attitudes of others.

The Football Factory John King, (Vintage, ISBN 009947462X)
A serious book that examines the world of football violence through its central character, Tom Johnson.

Different Seasons Stephen King, (Time Warner, ISBN: 0751504335)
A collection of four novellas, any one of which could be used for a personal study text. Two of the tales were made into the films *Stand by Me* and *The Shawshank Redemption*.

Cal Bernard MacLaverty, (Penguin Books, ISBN: 0140817891)
Set in the troubles of Northern Ireland this is a love story riddled with Cal's guilt. An accessible text for all students.

The Child in Time Ian McEwan, (Vintage, ISBN: 0099755017)
Examines the impact on a young couple of their child being snatched away from them.

Laidlaw William McIlvanney, (Sceptre, ISBN: 0340576901)
The first of McIlvanney's Laidlaw books in which the detective tracks down the murderer of a young girl, exploring various aspects of Glasgow life in the process. A good detective story as well as plenty of material to write about in an essay.

The Bluest Eye Toni Morrison, (Vintage, ISBN: 0099759918)
A young girl, Pecola, who longs for blue eyes like her white friends. A novel about identity from one of America's most powerful authors.

Sorrelle Millie Murray, (Livewire, ISBN: 070434954X)
Again from the *Livewire* series, about a young black woman and her Asian boyfriend and the problems they face from both families.

Not for Glory Janet Paisley, (Canongate, ISBN: 1841951749)
A series of interlinked stories set in a small village in central Scotland. Paisley examines the lives of a host of related characters through the unusual structure of this book.

Fight Club Chuck Palahniuk, (Vintage, ISBN 0099765217)
Quite a complex narrative and quite brutal in places. A challenging text.

Man and Boy Tony Parsons, (HarperCollins, ISBN: 0006512135)
The story of a father who has to learn how to care for his son after his own infidelity leads to the departure of his wife. A clever and accessible book about relationships and responsibilities.

My Story Dave Pelzer, (Orion, ISBN: 0752864017)
Pelzer's autobiographical trilogy, outlining the abuse he received as a child through to his eventual redemption, presented in one volume.

His Dark Materials Trilogy – The Northern Lights, The Subtle Knife and The Amber Spylass Philip Pullman, (Scholastic Press, ISBN: 0439994349)
Pullman's writing initially creates a world similar to our own but then expands out from there to encompass many others, challenging the reader to consider dominant morality and philosophy.

Tooth and Nail Ian Rankin, (Orion, ISBN: 0752809407)
Part of the *Rebus* series that is very popular at the moment. In this tale Rebus heads south to track down the 'Wolfman'.

Interview with the Vampire Anne Rice, (Ballantine Books, ISBN: 0345476875)
The first in a series of 'Vampire' books from Rice, this books explores the vampire legend in an accomplished and thought-provoking manner.

The Lovely Bones Alice Sebold, (Piccolo, ISBN 0330485385)
A young girl is murdered and then finds herself looking down from her own heaven as her family and friends try to cope with the aftermath.

Pygmalion George Bernard Shaw, (Penguin Books, ISBN: 0140437894)
Written to be read as well as acted, Pygmalion is the tale of Eliza Dolittle, a social experiment for two eminent gentlemen who wager about the possibility of turning this flower-girl into a lady. (Drama)

Touching the Void Joe Simpson, (Vintage, ISBN: 0099771012)
A story of the difficulties the author and his climbing partner faced on their descent from the top of the 21,000 foot Siula Grande mountain. Told from two perspectives, this is a gripping account of the challenges confronted in the face of death.

Men Should Weep Ena Lamont-Stewart, (Samuel French, ISBN: 0573018383)
A classic play set in the Glasgow of the past but still relevant to the Glasgow of today as it examines the role of women in the family and society generally. (Drama)

Anita and Me Meera Syal, (Flamingo, ISBN: 0006548768)
A memoir of growing up in the sixties when the author was part of the only Punjabi family in a small mining village. Humorous and skilfully told.

Oranges Are Not the Only Fruit Jeanette Winterson, (Orion, ISBN: 0099935708)
A young girl growing up in a deeply religious household struggles to come to terms with her own sexual orientation.

The Shadow of the Wind Carlos Ruiz Zafon, (Phoenix, ISBN 0753819317)
The discovery of a forgotten book leads to the hunt for its author – but things are not as they seem.

Gangsta Rap Benjamin Zephaniah, (Bloomsbury, ISBN 0747565651)
Excluded from school Ray develops an interest in music through a local project but when another rap band take a dislike to what he is doing, trouble soon flares.

Refugee Boy Benjamin Zephaniah, (Bloomsbury, ISBN 0747550867)
The story of Alem – abandoned in London by his father, who thinks that he will be safer there than back in war-torn Eritrea.

Index